Workshop on Annotation of Modal Meanings in Natural Language

(WAMM 2013)

Held at the 10th International Conference on Computational Semantics (IWCS 2013)

Potsdam, Germany
19 March 2013

ISBN: 978-1-62748-397-1

Printed from e-media with permission by:

Curran Associates, Inc.
57 Morehouse Lane
Red Hook, NY 12571

CURRAN ASSOCIATES INC.
proceedings
.com

Some format issues inherent in the e-media version may also appear in this print version.

Printed by Curran Associates, Inc. (2013)

For permission requests, please contact the Association for Computational Linguistics at the address below.

Association for Computational Linguistics
209 N. Eighth Street
Stroudsburg, Pennsylvania 18360

Phone: 1-570-476-8006
Fax: 1-570-476-0860

acl@aclweb.org

Additional copies of this publication are available from:

Curran Associates, Inc.
57 Morehouse Lane
Red Hook, NY 12571 USA
Phone: 845-758-0400
Fax: 845-758-2634
Email: curran@proceedings.com
Web: www.proceedings.com

TABLE OF CONTENTS

Challenges in Modality Annotation in a Brazilian Portuguese Spontaneous Speech Corpus 1
L. Avila, H. Mello

Analyzing Modal and Enunciative Discursive Heterogeneity: How to Combine Semantic Resources and a Syntactic Parser Analysis 7
D. Battistelli, M. Damiani

An Analysis of Disagreement-provoking Factors in the Analysis of Epistemic Modality and Evidentiality: the Case of English Adverbials 16
M. Carretero, J. Zamorano-Mansilla

Annotating Modal Expressions in the Chinese Treebank 24
Y. Cui, T. Chi

Influence of Modality Markers on the Conditional Interpretation of the German Preposition Ohne 33
C. Roch

Toward Fine-grained Annotation of Modality in Text 38
A. Rubinstein, H. Harner, E. Krawczyk, D. Simonson, G. Katz, P. Portner

Distant Annotation of Chinese Tense and Modality 47
N. Xue, Y. Zhang, Y. Yang

Challenges in modality annotation in a Brazilian Portuguese Spontaneous Speech Corpus

Luciana Beatriz Avila
PosLin-UFMG/UFV/Capes
Av Antonio Carlos 6627
Belo Horizonte, MG 31270-901 Brazil
lucianabeatrizavila@gmail.com

Heliana Mello
UFMG/FGV/CNPq
Av Antonio Carlos 6627
Belo Horizonte, MG 31270-901 Brazil
heliana.mello@gmail.com

Abstract

This short paper introduces the first notes about a modality annotation system that is under development for a spontaneous speech Brazilian Portuguese corpus (C-ORAL-BRASIL). We indicate our methodological decisions, the points which seem to be well resolved and two issues for further discussion and investigation.

1 Credits

The authors are thankful to CNPq, FAPEMIG and CAPES (Proc. nº BEX 9537/12-0) for research funding support.

2 Introduction

Modality annotation is inexistent for both written and spoken Brazilian Portuguese corpora, thus the novelty of this project. According to Nurmi (2007:1), linguistic annotation is helpful for the recovering of linguistic elements; however, the multifaceted nature of modality "is still a hurdle in computer assisted-research". Following up on the same reasoning, Baker et al. (2010: 1403) say that "[t]he challenge of creating a modality annotation scheme was to deal with the complex scoping of modalities with each other and with negation, while, at the same time creating a simplified operational procedure that could be followed by language experts without special training". Therefore, understanding what this semantic category stands for, as well as identifying linguistic elements that carry it, is of utmost relevance.

Our goal in annotating modality in a spontaneous speech Brazilian Portuguese Corpus is to provide a reliable starting point for researchers that might be interested in developing methodologies associated to NLP that ensue the extraction of oral discourse reliability, certainty and factuality markers, or carrying sentiment analysis, modeling modality and similar objectives.

3 Defining modality

In this paper we study modality in a spontaneous speech corpus, the C-ORAL-BRASIL, which will be presented in 4 below. As for spontaneous speech, we follow Cresti and Scarano (1998:5) in characterizing it as "the fulfillment of linguistic acts, not programmed and not programmable, because they emerge during the unfolding of an interaction, always new and unpredictable, between interlocutors." Their view is based on Austin's (1962) Speech Act Theory that associates spoken text to the realization of speech acts. According to Cresti and Scarano spontaneous speech is governed by an illocutionary principle, not found in written texts, as well as specific informational articulations.

Modality is taken here in Ballinian terms, that is, it stands for the evaluation or the point of view of a subject who evaluates the locutory material in a given utterance in a communicative act. Since the domain of our analysis is the spoken text, we follow Cresti's (2000) Language into Act Theory, whereby the utterance is the analytical reference unit that will be taken into consideration. This significantly differs from studies that rely on the sentence as the reference unit for the analysis of modality (eg. Fintel, 2006). An utterance carries an illocution and its locutory material does not necessarily carry a proposition. An utterance may be simple when comprised by one tone unit or complex when it is made up by two or more tone units. The scope of modality is the tone unit as proposed by Tucci (2007). Hence, within a given complex utterance, there might be different tone units which carry different modal values. When a tone unit carries more than one modal marker they may not share the same modal value, in which case the dominant modality will prevail. This can be appreciated in the examples below:

(i) REN: **se** a gente vai de táxi / voltar de táxi / **po'** comprar um //
If we go by taxi / come back by taxi / (you) may buy one //

In (i) there are three information units compounding a complex utterance. The first one carries epistemic modality while the last one carries deontic modality. Albeit belonging to the same utterance, the modalities that mark each information unit are not semantically compositional. Whereas in (ii) below, two modal values within the same information units will be compositional and the dominant value will prevail:

(ii) GIL:<eu **acho** que **tem que** ser esses> //
I think that it has to be these

In (ii) there is a single information unit, a Comment, which carries two modality indexes, *acho* "think", an epistemic marker, and *tem que* "have to", a deontic marker. The utterance in this case carries only one information unit and its modality is epistemic.

Modality in speech at times might get confused with other categories that carry subjective judgment; however a good rule of thumb to identify modal markers is to proceed to a semantic analysis leaving strictly pragmatic values aside. This has been demonstrated through an experiment reported in Mello and Raso (2011) who indicate the differentiation between modality, illocution and attitude in speech. Modality is related to the modus on dictum (Bally, 1942), illocution is the actum of the dictum, while attitude is the modus on actum. Therefore, modality can be classified as a semantic category, whereas both illocution and attitude are pragmatic notions. Modality, when marked, is carried by lexical and grammatical items on the one hand, while illocution and attitude are carried by prosodic cues.

In our work we focused on overt modal markers and took into consideration the following modal values: epistemic, deontic and dynamic. Epistemic modality refers to the conceptualizer's point of view, as far as possibility and necessity are concerned, in a given uttered material. This can be seen in the example below:

(iii) REN: **<pode> // tanto faz //** pode **//**
<It can be> // it doesn't matter // it can be //
FLA: ou cê **acha** muito **//**
Or do you think this is too much //
REN: uhn **//** acho **que não //**
Uhn // I don't think so //

In deontic modality the conceptualizer, a moral agent, refers to obligation, permission, contingent necessity in the uttered locutory material, as in (iv):

(iv) HMB: ela **tem que** falar / assim / de que que ela gosta //
She has to say / like/ what she likes //

As for dynamic modality, it includes ability and intention (will), that is, the conceptualizer's expression of capability, as in (v):

(v) ROG: eu acho que eu **consigo** &mar [/1] fazer isso //
I think I can do this //

Modality is usually codified by several morphological and grammatical forms, among them modal auxiliaries, adverbs, evaluative adjectives, periphrastic forms, propositional verbs and conditionals. These forms will be taken into consideration in the proposed annotation system whereas some less conventionalised items that might be becoming grammaticalized in spoken Brazilian Portuguese will not be annotated because they require further investigation.

Our annotation proposal is inspired by other systems previously explored for English (Baker et al., 2010; Matsuyoshi et al., 2010; Saurí et al., 2006, 2007; Szarvas et al., 2008) and it closely follows the scheme proposed by Hendrickx, Mendes and Mencarelli (2012) who explored modality annotation in European Portuguese (EP) speech.

The EP proposed scheme takes into account seven modal values and a number of corresponding subvalues, as shown in Table 1:

Values	Subvalues
Epistemic	knowledge belief doubt possibility interrogative
Deontic	obligation permission
Participant-internal	necessity: personal needs capacity: personal capacity
Evaluation	(evaluation of the proposition)
Volition	(hopes and wishes)
Effort	(attempt of the participant to make sth. happen)
Success	(results of the commitment of the participant)

Table 1 – European Portuguese selected modal values and subvalues

The system we advance here is more economical and reflects a canonical typology of modal meanings, as we show below. In both schemes (EP and BP), the three main categories overlap (Epistemic, Deontic, Dynamic or Participant-Internal), but it is not sufficiently clear so far whether a variety of non-epistemic meanings taken into consideration in the EP system should be considered as separate modal values, or rather as subvalues of Epistemic modality.

Other related works on modality annotation, accordingly to their goals, also present a range of modal values, denoting requirement, permissiveness, intention, ability, effort, success want and belief (Baker et al. 2010); assertion, volition, wish, imperative, permission, interrogative (Matsuyoshi et al. 2010); purpose, need, obligation and desire events (Morante & Daelemans, 2012).

Much of these works describes other components which are involved in the expression of modality, such as trigger, target and holder (Baker et al. 2010) or source, time, conditional, primary modality type, actuality, evaluation and focus (Matsuyoshi et al. 2010).

Following on the footsteps of the annotation scheme for EP, our proposal aims at contributing to the development of NLP projects, especially those based on spontaneous speech and its particularities.

4 A Brazilian Portuguese spontaneous speech corpus: the C-ORAL-BRASIL

C-ORAL-BRASIL follows the same architecture as the European Romance spontaneous spoken corpus C-ORAL-ROM (Cresti and Moneglia, 2005), whereby diaphasic variation is privileged in order for a large diversity of illocutions and informational structuring to be documented. C-ORAL-BRASIL comprises 200 texts of approximately 1,500 words each. Its informal half has been published (Raso and Mello, 2012) and exhibits a majority of private/familiar texts (80%) over public texts (20%), equally distributed into dialogues, conversations (3 or more participants) and monologues. The corpus follows the CHILDES-CLAN transcription format to which prosodic annotation is added, marking tone unit and utterance boundaries, besides several phenomena typical of speech. The entire corpus is speech to text aligned through use of WinPitch software.

5 Annotating modality in the C-ORAL-BRASIL

In this study a sample from the C-ORAL-BRASIL was taken into consideration. It covers 20 texts with an average of 1,500 words each, thereby totally 31,318 words; 5,484 utterances and 9,825 tone units. 1,155 modality marked tone units were found. The identification of modal markers was undertaken by three annotators working independently and qualitatively validated through group discussions. The search for modal markers was performed manually, through qualitative textual analysis, supported by the WinPitch software which allows for the concomitant examination of speech signal and transcription.

The data were organized in a table containing the modal markers, the tone unit in which they occurred, the type of information unit they are inserted in, the file they belong to, and any qualitative information deemed relevant.

The modality annotation scheme we propose takes into account The Language Into Act Theory and its reference unit, the utterance, and its subunits, that is, information units (Cresti, 2000). The scope of modality also follows the proposal established within that theory, thereby assigning its locus to the information unit (Tucci, 2007). Additionally, as mentioned, previous work on English and European Portuguese modality annotation is observed closely (cf. Section 3) in addition to opinion and emotions annotation (Wiebe et al., 2005).

The methodological steps taken in order for us to arrive at a modality annotation system were the following: the listing of a set of modal values emerging from the modal indexes found in the corpus; these values were subsequently tested on a sample of our subcorpus.

For the purpose of modality annotation we consider three modal values: epistemic, deontic and dynamic. As discussed above, epistemic modality relates to the conceptualizer's commitment to a given locutory material. Epistemic modality carries seven subvalues: knowledge, opinion, belief, possibility, probability, necessity and verification. [1] Deontic modality encompasses four subvalues: obligation, permission, prohibition and restriction. Finally, dynamic modality comprises three subvalues: ability, capacity and volition/intention.

In addition to modal values, the annotation scheme is made up of the following elements:

- **Trigger (M)**: the morpholexical and grammatical items that carry modality;
- **Source of the modality (src_mod)**: the conceptualizer, who might coincide with the speaker , the addressee, or another individual whose perspective and view point is being reported;
- **Source of the event mention (src_evt):** the producer**,** the speaker;
- **Target (T)**: the expression in the scope of the trigger within an annotation unit, that is, information units (IU)that carry modality (Comment, Topic, Parenthetical, Locutive Introducer), described in Table 2:

	IU	Information function
Textual units	Comment	Expresses the illocutionary force of the utterance
	Topic	Specifies the *locus* of application of the illocutionary force of the Comment
	Parenthetical	Expresses metalinguistic integration of the utterance
	Locutive Introducer	Signals pragmatic suspension of the *hic et nunc* and introduces a metaillocution

Table 2 – Modalized textual units (Cresti, 2000)[2]

An example of a modality annotated utterance is given below. Due to space constrains, we cannot discuss all the details involved in the process, however, it is relevant to note the following: elements within = marks stand for information unit labeling, angled brackets stand for speech overlaps, square brackets stand for modality annotated elements, single slashes stand for non-terminal breaks and double slashes for terminal breaks.

(vi) EVN$_{S1}$: é / [a <gente]$_{S1}$ [tem que]$_{M}$> <[restringir também]$_{T}$ / isso> //
Yeah / we have to restrict too / this //

The annotated elements are the following:

Trigger	tem que
Source of modality	A gente, 1p
Source of event mention	EVN
Modal value	deontic_obligation
Target	restringir também

Example (vi) is very straightforward and leaves no room for discussion as far as modality labeling

[1] We include here factuality and certainty features.

[2] Adapted from Tucci (2007).

and domains are concerned. However, this is not all we see in the data analyzed. There is plenty for discussion regarding some complex issues. Two of these are briefly mentioned below.

One of the challenges is the characterization of the elements that fulfill the role of Source. In our sample we found a majority of cases in which the conceptualizer overlaps with the first person speaker (cf. vi). However, there are cases in which the speaker presupposes or evaluates the kind of modal judgment that is made by others, in which case apparently there could be two conceptualizers, whereby two Source roles would be assigned, S_1 and S_2 and the assigned modal value would be shared by them (cf. vii). Yet another case occurs when the speaker reports the modal judgment made by a third party, in which case, the speaker does not partake in the modal conceptualization that is overtly manifested (cf. viii).

(vii) **JOR**$_{\mathbf{S1}}$: se o brasileiro nũ lê os manuais /=TOP= hhh no mercado de reposição / &auto [/1] de autopeça / **eles**$_{\mathbf{S2}}$ acham que abrir uma empresa é comprar um produto por um real / na base cem / e vender por dois acha que tá ganhando o &do [/2] o dobro //

If Brazilians don't read manuals / ..../ **they** think that to open a business is to buy a product by one real/ .../ and to sell it for two (they) think they are making double //

(viii) **PAU**: e **a Isa**$_{\mathbf{S1}}$ tava achando que ela ali ia ficar pequena //

And **Isa** was thinking that it would be small //

These two last examples lead us to mark up two different sources, following the annotation scheme proposed by Hendrickx, Mendes and Mencarelli (2012): Source of the event mentioned and Source of the modality. The first one corresponds to the producer of the sentence with the modal marker; the second one to the person who is agent/experiencer of modality.

As pointed out by Saurí et al.'s FactBank annotation scheme (Saurí, 2008; Saurí and Pustejovsky, 2009), there is always a default source[3] corresponding to the author of the text and "the factuality value assigned to events in text must be relative to the relevant sources at play in the discourse [...]" (Saurí and Pustejovsky, 2009, p. 240).

In (vii), we have at least two different event mentions[4] introduced by modal markers (e_1, by "se", and e_2, by the epistemic verb "achar"). The difference between event e_1 and event e_2 is that in e_1 the Source of the modality and the Source of the event mentioned overlap ("JOR") and refer to the epistemic judgment expressed by the conditional construction, whereas in e_2 Source of the event mentioned ("JOR") and Source of the modality ("eles") are different entities. The relation between S1 and the epistemic judgment of S2 is based on a supposition on the evaluation of the second conceptualizer, not necessarily corresponding to the truth-value of the uttered material.

Finally, in (viii), Source of the modality ("a Isa") and Source of the event mentioned ("PAU") are explicitly distinct. There is just the third-person conceptualizer, "a Isa", and her epistemic judgment is reported by "PAU".

A second challenge is presented by the labeling of target. In default circumstances, the target shares the same information unit as the modal marker, as posited by the Language into Act Theory, and which can be seen in the examples previously presented. However, there are cases in which there seems to be a percolation of the target through information unit boundaries, as if it were an anaphoric element, as can be seen in (ix) below:

(ix) GIL: <ô / mas> / voltando à questão / falando em e também falando em povo mascarado / esse povo do Galáticos é muito palha / eu [**acho que**]$_{\mathbf{M}}$ [es nũ deviam mais participar / e <tal>]$_{\mathbf{T}}$ //

(...) / I think that they shouldn't participate anymore / like //

LEO: <[**com certeza**]>$_{\mathbf{M}}$ //
Certainly //

[3] "Sources are understood here as the cognitive individuals presented as holding a specific stance with regards to the factuality status of events in text." (Saurí, 2008, p. 58).

[4] An event mention is defined as "consisting of a core predicate and its arguments (complements and adjuncts) in the sentence." (Matsuyoshi et al., 2010, p. 1458).

In the above example, "com certeza" refers back to the deontic assertion made in the previous turn "es nũ deviam mais participar"; however it is not clear how this can be annotated within the present scheme. One possible solution could be to add a Comment slot, in which we annotate the anaphoric reference.

6 Final remarks

In this short paper we have introduced the first notes about a modality annotation system that is being developed for a Brazilian Portuguese spontaneous speech corpus. Although we were able to point to some efficient methodological solutions we have implement so far, much remains open for discussion and further investigation.

.

References

Baker, K., Bloodgood, M., Dorr, B. J., Filardo, N. W., Levin, L., Piatko, C. 2010. A modality lexicon and its use in automatic tagging, in Proceedings of the Seventh Language Resources and Evaluation Conference (LREC'10).

CHILDES - Child Language Data Exchange System. Available at: http://childes.psy.cmu.edu/ Accessed: 29 Nov. 2012.

Cresti, E. 2000. *Corpus di italiano parlato*. Firenze: Accademia della Crusca.

Cresti, E.; Scarano, A. Sur la notion de parlé spontané. Available at: http://lablita.dit.unifi.it/preprint/preprint-98coll03.pdf. Accessed: 15 Nov. 2012.

Cresti, E.; Moneglia, M. 2005. *C-ORAL ROM*: Integrated reference corpora for spoken Romance languages. Amsterdam/Philadelphia: John Benjamins.

Hendrickx, I.; Mendes, A.; Mencarelli, S. Modality in Text: a Proposal for Corpus Annotation. in Proceedings of the Eighth conference on the International Language Resources and Evaluation (LREC'12), pp.1805-1812.

von Fintel, K. Modality and Language. In Encyclopedia of Philosophy – Second Edition, edited by Donald M. Borchert. Detroit: MacMillan Reference USA.

Martin, P. WinPitch Corpus. Available at: http://www.winpitch.com. Accessed: 15 Nov. 2012.

Matsuyoshi, S., Eguchi, M., Sao, C., Murakami, K., Inui, K., Matsumoto, Y. 2010, Annotating Event Mentions in Text with Modality, Focus, and Source Information, in Proceedings of the Seventh conference on the International Language Resources and Evaluation (LREC'10).

Mello, H. R.; Raso, T. 2011. Illocution, modality, attitude: different names for different categories. In: Mello, H. R.; Panunzi, A.; Raso, T (eds.). *Pragmatics and prosody*: illocution, modality, attitude, information patterning and speech annotation. Firenze: Firenze University Press, pp. 1-18.

Morante, R.; Daelemans, W. 2012. Annotating modality and negation for a machine reading evaluation. In: P. Forner, J. Karlgren, & C. Womser-Hacker (eds.), CLEF 2012 Conference and Labs of the Evaluation Forum - Question Answering For Machine Reading Evaluation (QA4MRE), Rome, Italy.

Nurmi, A. Employing and elaborating annotation for the study of modality. Available at: www.helsinki.fi/varieng/journals/volumes/01/nurmi/ . Accessed: 27 Mar. 2012.

Raso, T.; Mello, H. 2012. *C-ORAL-BRASIL I*: Corpus de referência do português brasileiro falado informal e DVD multimedia. Belo Horizonte: Editora UFMG,. v. 1.

Saurí, R., Verhagen, M., Pustejovsky, J. 2006. Annotating and recognizing event modality in text, in Proceedings of the 19th International FLAIRS Conference, FLAIRS 2006.

Saurí, R. 2008. A Factuality Profiler for Eventualities in Text. Ph.D. Thesis. Brandeis University.

Saurí, R., J. Pustejovsky. 2009. FactBank: A Corpus Annotated with Event Factuality. Language Resources and Evaluation. Available at: http://link.springer.com/article/10.1007/s10579-009-9089-9/fulltext.html. Accessed: 28 jan. 2013.

Szarvas, G., Vincze, V., Farkas, R., Csirik, J. 2008. The BioScope corpus: annotation for negation, uncertainty, and their scope in biomedical texts, in Proceedings of the Workshop on Current Trends in Biomedical Natural Language Processing, Association for Computational Linguistics, pp. 38-45.

Tucci, I. 2007. La modalità nel parlato spontaneo e il suo dominio de pertinenza. Una ricerca corpus-based (C-ORAL-ROM italiano). Actes du XXVe CILPR. (Innsbruk 3-8 September 2007). Available at: http://lablita.dit.unifi.it/preprint/preprint.2008-02-06.3658867998 Accessed: 13 jan. 2013.

Wiebe, J., Wilson, T., Cardie, C. 2005. Annotating expressions of opinions and emotions in language. Kluwer Academic Publishers, pp. 1-54.

Analyzing modal and enunciative discursive heterogeneity: how to combine semantic resources and a syntactic parser analysis

Delphine Battistelli
Université Paris Sorbonne,
STIH, EA 4509
Paris, F-75006, France
delphine.battistelli@paris-sorbonne.fr

Marine Damiani
Université Paris Ouest,
MoDyCo, UMR 7114
Nanterre, F-92000, France
marinedamiani@gmail.com

Abstract

This paper introduces our methodology for annotating variations in enunciative and modal commitment in a text. We first present the theoretical background of the study which puts the emphasis on the close interaction between time, aspect, modality and evidentiality (TAME) categories (and also markers). We then present our semantic resources which encompass not only lexical items, but also morphological inflections and syntactic constructions. We finally describe the first step of our global natural language processing (NLP) workflow which uses a syntactic analysis parser.

1 Introduction

Our paper concerns the design and development of lexical and grammatical resources for French in order to annotated textual segments in texts with regard to their modal and enunciative characteristics. The present study is part of a broader project (named *ChronoLines*[1]) which deals with the generation of innovative interfaces to display information according to temporal criteria from newswire texts in French provided by the Agence France Presse (AFP). The main goal of this project is closely related to applications such as the construction of timelines from texts (e.g. Alonso and al. 2009); its originality, however, compared to current timelines, is that we aim to take explicitly into account the problem of different levels of temporal referencing. These levels are associated with the different strategies to manage enunciative and modal expression which can be identified within the texts. Along similar lines to the annotation of "attributions" and "private states" (Wilson and Wiebe, 2005) or the calculation of "factuality degrees of events" (Sauri and Pustejovsky, 2012), we aim to take into account the fact that, independently of their calendar anchoring, situations can be presented as certain, fully accomplished, or only possible/probable, by an enunciator who can be the author of the text but who can also be another enunciator (explicitly named or not) from whom the author reports some content that he has heard, read, imagined. ... It should be noted that around 90% of newswire text sentences contain at least one clue of an epistemic modal and/or enunciative shift.

In section 2, we present the theoretical background of the study. Section 3 details our methodology for detecting variations in enunciative and modal commitment in a text (via the detection of certain lexical and grammatical cues, including certain kinds of syntactic constructions) and then identifying embedded textual segments which correspond to these shifts/variations (thanks to a syntactic parser analysis). Section 4 describes the first step of our global natural language processing (NLP) methodology.

2 Theoretical background: *modality meaning* and TAME categories

The notion of modality, which is closely linked to the notion of evidentiality[2], has been studied from

[1] The ChronoLines project is funded by the French National Research Agency (ANR-10-CORD-010). http://chronolines.fr/

[2] This notion is implied when a new source of information is introduced in the discourse (reported, hearsay, inferred,...).

many different perspectives: logic, philosophy and linguistics - see for example (Bybee and al., 1994; Palmer, 2001; Nuyts, 2006). In the field of linguistics, modality can be considered from an enunciative perspective - see (Bally, 1935; Benveniste, 1966; Culioli, 1973). From this perspective, which is the one we adopt here, the construction of an utterance (or a text) has to take into account certain language operations such as predication, discourse operations and operations of commitment[3], the expression of which leaves a certain number of surface linguistic traces (or clues). The enunciator's degree of commitment to a predicative content introduces variations in aspect, time and modality and also what is called enunciative modalities, all marked in the utterance by traces that the enunciator leaves in the discourse. In the case of direct speech, these traces can manifest themselves in the introductory portion of the direct reported speech in different forms: they may indicate the enunciator's stance towards what is reported, describe the speaker's attitude towards what is being said (in general) or towards what the speaker himself is saying; or refer to the relationship between the speaker and the enunciator, etc. The linguistic act of reported speech permits the enunciator to indicate his/her commitment to what is said or written by another source. Thus, what is emphasized in an enunciative perspective is the intrinsic presence of the enunciator in every discourse production. This presence is mainly manifested via time, aspect, modal and/or evidential traces. These four kinds of linguistic traces refer to four kinds of intrinsically linked semantic categories (see the well-known acronym TAME). When only the categories of modality and evidentiality are considered, it can be said that the enunciator expresses different degrees of commitment to the truth of the propositional content.

At an analytical and descriptive level, which is essential in annotation tasks, and which is, moreover, sensitive to a specific language, several questions arise:

- what kinds of linguistic markers (even if they are most of the time ambiguous) can be considered as prototypical for each of the TAME categories (let's see for example "modal verbs" (*as must, …*), "hedging adverbs" (*as probably*), "reported speech verbs" *(as to say or to tell*), …)?
- how can markers that encode semantic instructions belonging to several TAME categories be handled? For example, certain tenses can play a role at all TAME levels - see for example (de Haan 1999, Hassler, 2010)
- how can the four (cognitivo-linguistic) operations that TAME categories refer to be ordered - see (Dik, 1997)?
- how can a textual perspective of TAME categories be taken into account, that is to say how can these categories be explored beyond the syntactic level of utterances? This problem has been very rarely addressed in theoretical linguistics and in NLP approaches – see for example (Battistelli, 2011)
- how should one deal with the problem of the interaction of different epistemic modality markers, at a sentence level – see (Sauri et Pustejovsky, 2012) - and at a textual level? Note that this question directly leads to the question of possibly different levels of predication. Let's take the case of sentence level. One sentence frequently expresses more than one situation (predicative content) and each of the situations can be qualified with a different degree of certainty;
- how can one deal with the problem, closely linked to the previous one, of the scope of modality markers, and therefore of the length of "modalised" textual segments?

In order to analyze the highly complex interaction between the categories of modality and evidentiality, our methodology first focuses on detecting these "modalised" textual segments and on analyzing their hierarchical organization. This is what we choose to present in this paper.

From our enunciative perspective, this leads us to take a look at the text in its enunciative and/or

[3] The term of commitment is a close counterpart to the French term "prise en charge" – see (De Brabanter and Dendale, 2008).

modal variations. Indeed, throughout a text (even within a single sentence), enunciative and modal values tend to vary. For example, encountering a reporting verb such as *dire/to say*, *répondre/to answer*, *annonce/to announce*, introduces a variation in the enunciative value but no variation in the modal value; an adverb such as sûrement/ probably, *probablement/likely*, introduces a variation in the modal value; a verb such as *prétendre/to claim*, *croire/to believe*, *imaginer/to imagine*, introduces a variation in both the modal and the enunciative value.
In the next section, we detail the methodology developed to analyze these variations.

3 Methodology for analyzing discursive heterogeneity by detecting E_M segments

Any discourse (and by extension even a discourse comprising a single sentence) is necessarily presented from the viewpoint of a human cognizer (in our case, the journalist who writes the newswire). Thus, any discourse always has a default source who is its author. Moreover, as explained in the previous section, we consider modality from an enunciative perspective. Any newswire can then be considered as a textual segment having "default" enunciative (= 'author') and modal (= 'true', based on the Gricean maxim of quality which testifies that sources are trustworthy) values. Most of the time, in a text (even within a single sentence), textual segments which have different enunciative and modal values can be identified. This is due to the complex mechanisms of interaction between semantic clues that we outlined in section 2.
Our methodology consists in focusing on the tracking on semantic clues which have to be taken into account in order to identify different enunciative and modal textual segments. This kind of approach to modal meaning focuses on discursive heterogeneity and also makes it possible to deal with the interaction between Modality and other related linguistic categories (Time, Aspect and Evidentiality). Furthermore, we believe that developing such an approach could - beyond the applicative interest in information retrieval (cf. *ChronoLines* already mentioned) - help to achieve a better understanding of this complex TAME interaction at a discursive level, i.e. at a level where pertinent textual units are not only sentences or utterances. In the remainder of the article, we will give just examples of sentences, but we wish to emphasize that our methodology also enables a discourse level analysis.
We propose to set up a NLP workflow (see Fig. 1) that automates the annotation process of the text into textual segments that have enunciative and modal features. These textual segments will be called from now on E_M segments. In this workflow, we distinguish two main steps:
Step 1: concerns the E_M splitter module which produces annotation of a text as a succession or imbrication of E_M segments. It uses semantic clues (organized in E_M semantic resources database) that lead to the opening of new E_M segments; it also uses a syntactic parser to calculate the length of an E_M segment at the sentence level;
Step 1bis: aims at linking different sentences in a single E_M segment if they denote a homogeneous discourse unit;
Step 2: the E_M value assigner determines the values of E_M segments. Semantic clues are again used insofar as some of them have an influence only on the enunciative value of an E_M segment, or only on its modal value, or on both its enunciative and modal value.

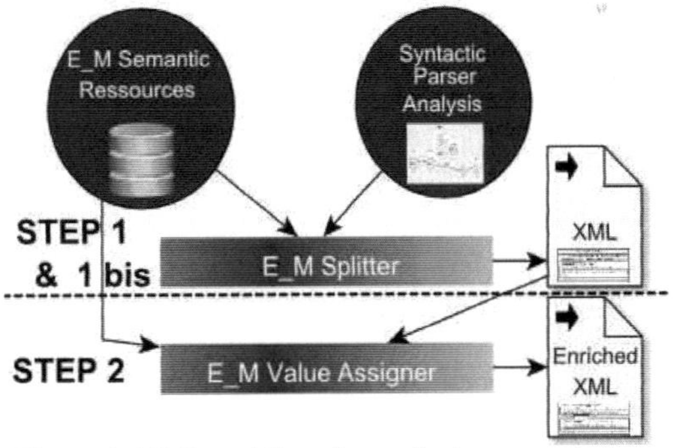

Figure 1. NLP workflow for analyzing enunciative and modal discursive heterogeneity

Figure 2 shows as embedded boxes the E_M segments (from 'E_M_1_dft' to 'E_M_4') that we want the final system to produce for the sentence in example 1. The involved semantic clues (from c=1 to 3) are highlighted.

1. *La Syrie a nié jeudi avoir fourni au Hezbollah libanais des missiles Scud capables d'atteindre l'ensemble du territoire israélien, accusant l'Etat*

hébreu de vouloir, avec de telles accusations, faire monter la tension au Proche-Orient. (*Syria denied on Thursday having supplied the Lebanese Hezbollah with Scud missiles capable of reaching the whole territory of Israel, accusing the Hebrew State of seeking, through such charges, to heighten tension in the Middle East.*)

'E_M_1_dft' is the "default" segment. Over the text, every occurrence of a linguistic clue "opens" a new E_M segment. We will see later how we identify the length of each E_M segment depending on the different types of linguistic clues. For now, we can say that clue 1 *a nié/denied* opens segment 'E_M_2' and that clue 2 "accuser/to accuse" opens segment 'E_M_3'. Finally, clue3 *vouloir/seeking* opens segment 'E_M_4'. As can be seen, an E_M segment can follow another E_M segment (for example 'E_M_3' follows 'E_M_2') or be embedded in another E_M segment (for example 'E_M_4' is embedded in 'E_M _3').

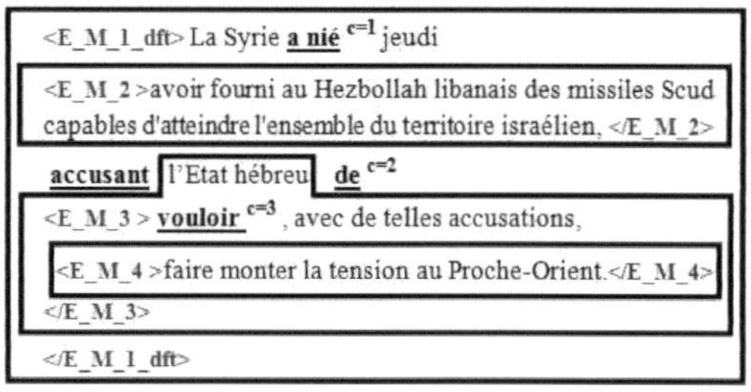

Figure 2. Example of an E_M splitter output4

In the next section, we detail Step1 and then focus on the building of semantic resources and the relevance of using a syntactic parser to identify E_M segments. Step1bis and Step2 will be dealt with in other papers.

4 Using semantic resources and a syntactic parser analysis to detect E_M segments

The identification of an E_M segment in the text is, as we have just seen, founded on the tracking of semantic clues that open a new segment. In other words, every variation in the enunciative and/or modal meaning introduces a new E_M segment. Section 4.1 describes the organization of semantic resources and illustrates them with some examples. Then in section 4.2 we explain how we use the syntactic analysis produced by the parser.

4.1 Semantic resources

Semantic clues that are able to open a new E_M segment can be (see Fig. 3): lexical items (verbs of propositional attitude, speech verbs, nouns, adverbs, etc.), morphological inflections (for example tense inflections like in French *conditionnel* and *imparfait* tenses5), or specific syntactic constructions (subordinate clauses of condition, prepositional constructions). All kinds of them are used during Step1 in order to detect and split E_M segments. Note that these resources are also organized in the database at a deeper level in order to be used during Step2 to calculate the precise E_M segments values.

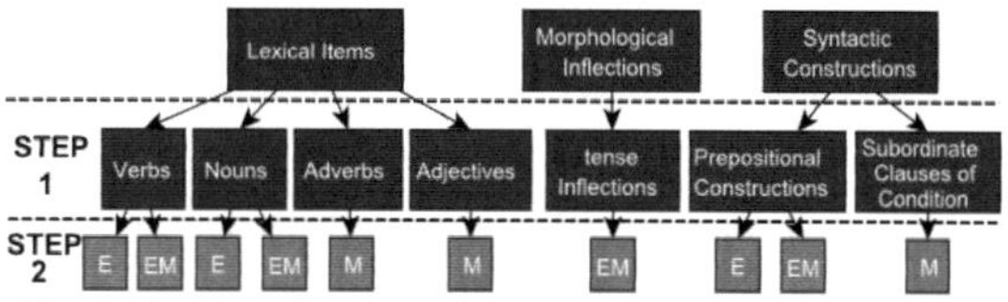

Figure 3. Organization of E_M semantic resources: at a surface level and at a deeper level

Lexical items

Lexical clues can be split into two groups: predicative clues and modifier clues.

- *Predicative clues: verbs and nouns*

A predicative clue introduces a new E_M segment which includes all the syntactic dependents of the predicate. These two categories of predicative clues involve a semantic variation: at the enunciative level (see example (2), where the clue *dire/says* introduces a new enunciative source for the E_M segment *Jean viendra/Jean will come*); or at both the enunciative and modal levels (see example (3) where the clue *pense/thinks* introduces both a new source and a modal variation). Example (4) illustrates the case of a sequence of several clues: clue1 *a exprimé/expresses* opens segment "E_M1" and influences only the modal validation context. Inside this segment, clue2 *le souhait/a*

[4] Note that the purpose of this representation as interlocking boxes is to illustrate our methodology; the actual annotation is in XML.

[5] See respectively (Kronning, 2002) and (De Mulder and Vetters, 2002).

desire impacts on both the enunciative and the modal validation context of segment "E_M2".

2. [Paul **dit**^{clue} que [Jean viendra]$_{E\_M}$]$_{E\_M\_dft}$. ([Paul **says**^{clue} that [Jean will come]$_{E\_M}$]$_{E\_M\_dft}$)

3. [Paul **pense**^{clue} que [Jean viendra]$_{E\_M}$]$_{E\_M\_dft}$. ([Paul **thinks**^{clue} that [Jean will come]$_{E\_M}$]$_{E\_M\_dft}$)

4. [M. Arabi **a exprimé**^{clue1} [**le souhait**^{clue2} [d'aider la Syrie à surmonter cette phase]$_{E\_M}$]$_{E\_M}$]$_{E\_M\_dft}$ ([Mr. Arabi **expressed**^{clue1} [**a desire**^{clue2} [to help Syria overcome this difficult.]$_{E\_M2}$]$_{E\_M}$]$_{E\_M\_dft\ 1}$)

- *Modifier clues: adverbs and adjectives*

Unlike predicative clues, modifier clues do not open a new E_M segment, but will modify the value of the current E_M segment during Step2. Sentence (5) is an example of this phenomenon: the clue *peut-être/may* directly modifies the predicate *viendra/come*. The modal value of the whole segment is then impacted.

5. [Jean viendra **peut-être**^{clue}]$_{E\_M\_dft}$. ([Jean **may** ^{clue} come]$_{E\_M\_dft}$.)

An adverb can also modify a verbal predicate which itself introduces an E_M segment. In this case, the adverb will not modify the value of the current E_M segment but the value of the E_M segment opened by the verbal predicate. Example (6) illustrates this case: clue2 *apparemment/apparently* impacts on clue1 *dit/says*. The value of the E_M segment will change at the enunciative level because of clue1, and at the modal level because of clue2.

6. [Paul **dit**^{clue1} **apparemment**^{clue2} que [Jean viendra]$_{E\_M}$]$_{E\_M\_dft}$. ([Paul **says**$^{clue\ 1}$ **apparently**^{clue2} that [Jean will come]$_{E\_M}$]$_{E\_M\_dft}$)

- *Building lexical resources*

The development of these lexical resources is based on the most frequent lexical items that occur in press AFP newswires. To find these most frequent items, we used a corpus of 20,000 texts (from the years 2010 and 2011). We then generated the frequency of the lemmatized corpus to find the most frequent lexical items. Our goal is to build resources that can cover at least 80% of the corpus. This coverage is reached with the 320 most frequent verbs. From this list of 320 verbs, we manually sorted 140 verbs which introduce a modal and/or an enunciative variation. We used the same technique to build the list of 15 adverbs and the list of 10 adjectives. For predicative nouns, we had to use another method because the number of nouns was too high and we also wanted to keep only predicative nouns. To solve this issue, we used Verbaction [6] which is a lexicon of nouns morphologically related to verbs. For each of our 140 verbs, we searched whether a related noun existed in Verbaction (this task has been automated). We obtained a list of nouns which can potentially be clues but the results then had to be manually filtered as some items were irrelevant for our work. For example Verbaction gives two predicative nouns coming from the verb *accepter/to accept*: *acceptation/acceptance* and *acception/acceptation*, and we decided to keep only the first noun (*acceptation/acceptance*). After this filtering process, the list of predicative nouns comprised 80 items. Let's mention we are currently still exploring additional resources, in particular by integrating syntactic and semantic information about verbs from (Hadouche and Lapalme, 2010).

Morphological inflections

Several morphological inflections in French form another type of clue implied in the opening of a new E_M segment; for example, the French conditional tense, which has the morphological inflection (*-rais, -rais,-rait,-rions,-riez,-raient*). This tense is prototypical of French journalistic practice. It introduces uncertainty about the source of the information and/or about the epistemic modal status of the information.

In example (7), the verb form *aurait annoncé/would have announced*[7] is composed of two clues. The clue *annoncé/announced* introduces a new enunciative source 'Jean' (distinct from the journalist source). The other clue is the morphological inflection "-rait". This morpheme is interpreted as a trace of the journalist's lack of commitment: the hearer/reader interprets this trace as an ambiguity marker concerning the true source of information (is it 'Jean' or someone else who

[6] http://redac.univtlse2.fr/lexicons/verbaction.html

[7] The verb form 'would have + verb' is the literal translation of the French pattern. A correct translation would be *Jean is said to have announced*.

announced…?) and/or the modal status of the E_M segment *le départ de Paul/Paul's departure*.

The ambiguity about the origin of the uncertainty (which can be enunciative and/or modal) implied by the use of the French *conditionnel* tense comes across particularly clearly when we look at the possible translations of the sentence in English. The translation we have chosen (*Jean is said to have announced Paul's departure*) shows that the ambiguity concerns the source and not the epistemic value of *le départ de Paul/Paul's departure*. However, this interpretation really depends on the context and it is often difficult in French to decide which of the two interpretations is intended. We will therefore simply consider that the French *conditionnel* tense leads to the opening of a new E_M segment, with indetermination concerning the origin of the journalist's lack of commitment.

7. [Jean **aurait**$^{\text{clue1}}$ **annoncé**$^{\text{clue2}}$ [le départ de Paul.]$_{\text{E\_M}}$]$_{\text{E\_M\_dft}}$ ([Jean **is said**$^{\text{clue1}}$ **to have announced**$^{\text{clue2}}$ [Paul's departure.]$_{\text{E\_M}}$]$_{\text{E\_M\_dft}}$)

Syntactic constructions

The third class of clues contains syntactic constructions which are able to open E_M segments.

- *Subordinate clauses of condition*

A subordinate clause of condition indicates in which conditions the propositional content of the main clause is realized. The main clause is therefore considered as an E_M segment and the subordinate clause as a semantic (modal) clue. In example (8), the subordinate clause *si Paul n'accepte pas/if Paul does not accept* acts as a clue opening the E_M segment associated to the main clause. Example (9) shows a similar case with a subordinate clause introduced by the conjunction *à condition de/on condition that*.

8. [[Marie a refusé de donner son accord]$_{\text{E\_M}}$ **si Paul n'accepte pas**$^{\text{clue1}}$]$_{\text{E\_M\_dft}}$.([[Mary refused to give her approval]$_{\text{E\_M}}$ **if Paul does not accept**$^{\text{clue1}}$]$_{\text{E\_M\_dft}}$)

9. [[Marie acceptera]$_{\text{E\_M}}$ **à condition que Paul vienne**$^{\text{clue1}}$]$_{\text{E\_M\_dft}}$ ([[Marie will accept]$_{\text{E\_M}}$ **on condition that Paul comes** $^{\text{clue1}}$]$_{\text{E\_M\_dft}}$

- *The prepositional constructions*

A prepositional construction such as selon X /according to X can also be considered as a semantic (enunciative) clue. Placed or not at the beginning of a sentence, this kind of expression introduces a new source and thus opens a new E_M segment, as illustrated in example (10). Another propositional construction such as à première vue/at the first sight can be considered as a semantic (enunciative and/or modal) clue.

10. [**Selon Paul**$^{\text{clue1}}$, [Jules vient]$_{\text{E\_M}}$]$_{\text{E\_M\_dft}}$ ([**According to Paul**$^{\text{clue1}}$, [Jules is coming]$_{\text{E\_M}}$)]$_{\text{E\_M\_dft}}$

11. [**A première vue**$^{\text{clue1}}$, [Marie a raison]$_{\text{E\_M}}$]$_{\text{E\_M\_dft}}$ ([**At first sight**, [Marie is right]$_{\text{E\_M}}$]$_{\text{E\_M\_dft}}$)

4.2 Using syntactic parser analysis to detect E_M segments boundaries

A semantic (modal and/or enunciative) clue is linked to an E_M segment: either the semantic clue opens a new E_M segment or it modifies the (modal and/or enunciative) value of the current E_M segment. In this section, we address the issue of defining the boundaries of E_M segments, using a syntactic parser. We use a large-coverage syntactic parser for French, FRMG (FRench MetaGrammar) (De La Clergerie et al., 2009). The main syntactic contexts in which semantic clues can occur are as follows:

- clausal complements (*Paul* ***dit*** *que…/Paul* ***says*** *that…*)
- adverbial clause modifiers (*Paul viendra* ***s'il ne pleut pas****/Paul will come* ***if it is not raining***)
- constructions with subject inversion (*"Marie va venir",* ***a dit Paul****/"Marie will come", **said Paul***)
- direct and indirect objects (*Paul* ***a demandé*** *l'intervention de la police/Paul* ***asked*** *the police to intervene*)
- verb modifiers (*Il est venu **mardi**/He came on **Tuesday***).
- noun complements (*Ceci est* ***le souhait de ces pays d'être impliqués****/This is* ***the wish of these countries to be involved***)

- relative clauses (*Il a exprimé* ***l'espoir que la guerre finisse****/He expressed* ***the hope that the war would end***)

From the observation of all these kinds of contexts, we have developed the general rule RULE_G1 which makes it possible to delimit an E_M segment: if a new E_M segment has been opened due to the presence of one predicative clue, then all the complements of this predicative clue except its modifiers [8] (e.g. temporal modifiers, purpose clause modifiers, etc.) are part of this new E_M segment. Furthermore, since any text (taken as a whole) is considered as an E_M segment having "default" enunciative and modal features, the text is always associated to E_M_1_dft and this constitutes the second general rule RULE_G2.

To illustrate the application of these two general rules, let's return to the example of sentence (1) given above. Figure 2 illustrates both the syntactic relations produced by the parser (shown by arrows) and the semantic clues implied in the analysis (shown in dotted lines). The dotted boxes delimit the E_M segments we want the system to detect.

In the case of figure 2, the text comprises a single sentence, and is thus associated to E_M_1_dft (RULE_G2). The semantic clue1 *a nié/denied* marks the opening of a new segment named E_M_2. The length of this segment depends on syntactic information coming from the parser. According to RULE_G1, this segment is composed of the clausal complement *avoir fourni au Hezbollah libanais des missiles Scud capables d'atteindre l'ensemble du territoire israélien / having supplied the Lebanese Hezbollah with Scud missiles capable of reaching the whole territory of Israel*, and does not include the temporal modifier *jeudi/Thursday* nor the modifier clause *accusant l'Etat hébreu (…)/accusing the Hebrew State of (…)*. Those two components remain in the segment E_M_1_dft.

Clue2 *accusant de/accusing of* marks the opening of a new segment E_M_3 which is composed of its complements (RULE_G1): the direct objet of the verb *l'Etat hébreu/the Hebrew state* and the clausal complement *vouloir avec de telles accusations faire monter la tension au proche orient/seeking through such charges to heighten tension in the Middle East*. Clue 3 is the verb *vouloir/seeking*. This clue marks the opening of a new segment E_M_4 which is, according to RULE_G1, composed of the direct object of the verb *vouloir/seek*, i.e. *faire monter la tension au Proche-Orient/to heighten tension in the Middle East*, but excludes the modifier *avec de telles accusations/through such charges*.

The E_M segment splitting system we have started to develop (named E_M splitter) takes into account the two general rules described above. We are currently working on E_M value assigner module (see Fig. 1) which is dedicated to assign values to the E_M segments. This module uses the deeper level of semantic resources organization (see Fig. 3), that is to say the distinction between intrinsic modal and/or enunciative meaning of clues. It uses also a heritage mechanism able to apprehend segment embedding (and thus the interaction between several clues).

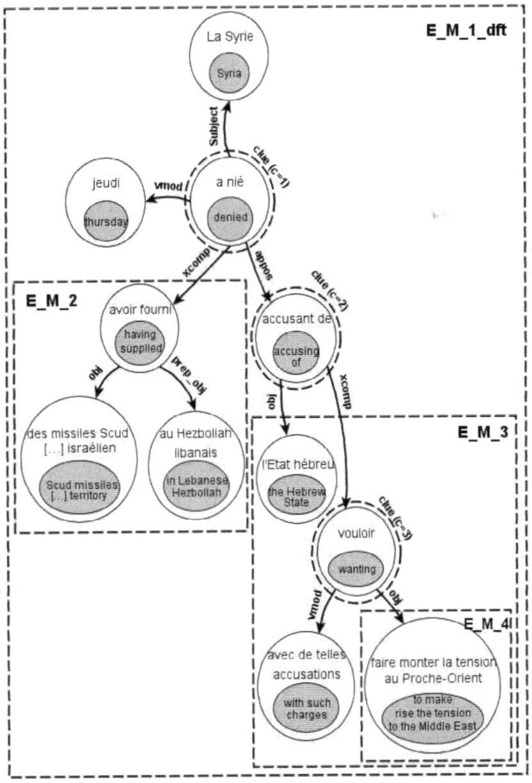

Figure 4. Using syntactic information to split E_M segments

[8] We decided to consider that, by default, information coming from modifiers has to be allocated to the writer and thus constitutes a form of textual background.

5 Conclusion

In this paper, we have focused on the different kinds of French resources that need to be involved in the annotation of textual segments according to - what is called in our enunciative theoretical background terminology - their enunciative and modal characteristics (hence the notion, and notation, of E_M segment). These two types of characteristics are involved both:

- in an information retrieval purpose (when dealing with - or calculating - the factual status of situations described in a text, as for example in certain textual entailment applications, or when dealing with attributions and polarity, as for example in opinion or sentiment analysis applications);
- and in a theoretical semantic purpose (when addressing the difficult matter of the shifting boundaries – either lexical or grammatical, and variously marked in different languages - between the notions of evidentiality and epistemic modality).

Thus, in the methodology that we have proposed to explore modal meaning and its annotation, the precise E_M characteristics are deliberately not addressed in the first step, but only in the second step (cf. Step 2 in Fig. 1), when the task of delimiting textual segments has already been approached (cf. Step 1 in Fig. 1). As we have seen, the present paper focuses on the problem of splitting a text into textual segments, and it presents how we envisage combining E_M semantic resources and a dependency syntactic analysis parser results to achieve segmentation.

We would like to point out that the way we build these semantic resources is quite original especially in an NLP perspective: firstly, because these resources encompass not only lexical items, but also morphological inflections and syntactic constructions (see section 4.1); secondly, because they aim to reflect some important theoretical investigations about the close interaction between TAME categories.

References

Alonso, O., Gertz, M. & Baeza-Yates, R. 2009. Clustering and exploring search results using timeline constructions. In Proceedings of the 18th ACM conference on Information and knowledge management (pp. 97-106).

Bally, C. 1932. Linguistique générale et Linguistique française. Paris : Leroux, 2éd. (1944), Berne.

Battistelli, D. 2011. Linguistique et recherche d'information. Hermès Publishing. Paris

Benveniste, E. 1966. Problèmes de linguistique générale, 1, Paris : Gallimard.

Bybee, J. L., Perkins, R., & Pagliuca, W. 1994. The evolution of grammar: tense, aspect and modality in the language of the world. University of Chicago Press.

De La Clergerie E., Sagot B., Nicolas L. et Guénot M. 2009. FRMG: évolutions d'un analyseur syntaxique TAG du français. In Journée ATALA "Quels analyseurs syntaxiques pour le français ?", Paris, France

Culioli, A. 1973. Sur quelques contradictions en linguistique. Communications , 20(1), 83-91.

De Brabanter, P., & Dendale, P. 2008. Commitment: The term and the notions. Belgian Journal of Linguistics , 22, 1-14.

De Haan, F. 1999. Evidentiality and epistemic modality. Setting boundaries. Southwest Journal of Linguistics, 18, 83-101.

De Mulder, W., & Vetters, C. 2002. The French imparfait, determiners and grounding. In F. Brisard (Éd.), Grounding: The Epistemic Footing of Deixis and Reference (pp. 113-149). Berlin/NY: Mouton de Gruyter.

Dik, S. C. 1997. The Theory of Functional Grammar. Part 1: The structure of clause (éd. Second). Berlin: Mouton de Gruyter.

Hadouche, F., & Lapalme, G. 2010. Une version électronique du LVF comparée avec d'autres ressources lexicales. Langages, 10(179-180), 193-220.

Hassler, G. 2010. Epistemic modality and evidentiality. Dans G. Diewald, & E. Smirnova (Éds.), Linguistic Realization of Evidentiality in European Languages (pp. 223-248). Berlin/NY: Mouton de Gruyter.

Nuyts, J. 2006. Modality: Overview and linguistic issues. In W. J. Frawley (Éd.), The Expression of Modality. Berlin: De Gruyter Mouton.

Palmer, F. 2001. Mood and Modality. Cambridge University Press.

Sauri, R., & Pustejovsky, J. 2012. Are You Sure That This Happened? Assessing the Factuality Degree of Events in Text. Computational Linguistics, 38(2), 261-299.

Wilson, T., & Wiebe, J. 2005. Annotating Attributions and Private States. In ACL 2005 Workshop: Frontiers in Corpus Annotation II: Pie in the Sky, (pp. 53-60).

An analysis of disagreement-provoking factors in the analysis of epistemic modality and evidentiality: the case of English adverbials

Marta Carretero
Departamento de Filología Inglesa I
Facultad de Filología
Universidad Complutense de Madrid
mcarrete@filol.ucm.es

Juan Rafael Zamorano-Mansilla
Departamento de Filología Inglesa I
Facultad de Filología
Universidad Complutense de Madrid
juanrafaelzm@filol.ucm.es

Abstract

This paper reports on a series of annotation experiments carried out on a number of English adverbials. The experiments, based on occurrences obtained from the British National Corpus, focused on the distinction of epistemic and evidential meanings from other kinds of meanings. The results led to the conclusion that many of the cases of inter-annotator disagreement were due to certain syntactic and semantic factors. Some of these factors will be described in detail, together with the decisions made in each case for prospective annotation.

1 Introduction

The annotation experiments described in this paper are part of the CONTRANOT project, aimed at the creation and validation of English-Spanish contrastive functional descriptions of a number of linguistic categories for corpus analysis and annotation [1]. As part of the corpus annotation activities developed in this project, in this paper we present some findings obtained during the process of annotating epistemic modality and evidentiality. More specifically, the paper describes work carried out on the initial stages of the coding system for the annotation of English epistemic and evidential adverbials: it includes an account of the initial coding system, together with an analysis of the most important factors that have given way to disagreement in the annotation of different adverbials. The analysis is mainly qualitative, due to the small number of examples analyzed, but the most relevant quantitative data have been specified.

The term 'adverbial', as it is used in this paper, encompasses adverbs such as *certainly, evidently* or *probably*, as well as expressions of other syntactic categories that are similar to them in meaning and function, such as the Noun Phrase *no doubt* or the Prepositional Phrases *in all probability, in all likelihood* or *for sure.*

The initial experiments that served to test the reliability of the coding scheme consisted in the annotation of 20 examples for each adverbial selected at random from the Brigham Young University version of the British National Corpus, available online at http://corpus.byu.edu/bnc/.

2 The coding system: the concept and scope of epistemic modality and evidentiality

The concept of epistemic modality adopted in this paper is in line with work based on modal logic, in which the different modal categories are treated in terms of possibility and necessity. [2] Accordingly,

[1] Data of the project: "Creation and validation of contrastive decriptions (English-Spanish) through corpus analysis and annotation: linguistic, methodological and computational issues". Ref. FFI2008-03384 (Ministry of Science and Innovation). Director: Prof. Julia Lavid, Universidad Complutense de Madrid.

[2] This approach is, perhaps, the most widely used for describing modal expressions in English. Some references are Hermerén (1978), Palmer (1990), Perkins (1983), Nuyts (2001), Wärnsby (2006) or Collins (2009).

epistemic modality is defined as the estimation of the probability for a proposition to have been, be or become true (cf. Nuyts 2001: 21). This concept of epistemic modality excludes certain expressions included in broader approches to epistemic modality, [3] which qualify the speaker/writer (sp/wr)'s commitment to the reliability of the information in different ways from probability in the strict sense: examples of these expressions are hedges of approximation (*sort of, or something...*) or stance adverbials of degree (*basically, essentially, totally*). These categories could well be the basis of parallel annotation systems in future.

As for evidentiality, it will be defined as the linguistic expression of the kind, source and/or evaluation of the evidence for or against the truth of the proposition that the sp/wr has at his/her disposal. We will consider it as a semantic category, in a similar way to Chafe (1986), not as a grammatical phenomenon as in Mithun (1986) or Anderson (1986), nor will we include cases in which evidentiality is pragmatically inferred (Ifantidou 2001).

The adverbials selected for this research meet the requirements of the scope of epistemic modality and evidentiality described above The list, which is not exhaustive in the present stage of this research, includes the following items:

- Epistemic adverbials of probability and possibility: *maybe, perhaps, probably, in all likelihood, in all probability, improbably, possibly, conceivably, plausibly* and *predictably.* [4]
- Epistemic adverbials of certainty: *assuredly, certainly, definitely, positively, surely, undeniably, unquestionably.*
- Evidential adverbials: *apparently, clearly, evidently, obviously, plainly.*

We believe that the evidential adverbials listed here, except for *apparently*, could be considered as epistemic and evidential at the same time, or 'epistentials', since they have an epistemic meaning of high degree of certainty (which is similar to that of the epistemic adverbials of certainty listed above) as well as an evidential meaning of sound evidence. However, we believe that, in spite of this overlap in the linguistic expression of epistemic modality and evidentiality, both categories should be kept separate in the annotation, in the sense that the consideration of the overlap would complicate matters. Consequently, all the adverbials with a semantic component of evidence will be considered as evidential, independently of whether they also have an epistemic semantic feature or not.

3 The experiments

The adverbials listed above were submitted to a first annotation experiment by two linguists knowledgeable about epistemic modality and evidentiality (concretely, the two authors of this paper), in which the epistemic and evidential meanings were to be distinguished from other meanings. That is to say, the tagging was restricted to a basic level, where the options were 'Epistemic/Non-epistemic' for the epistemic adverbials, and 'Evidential/Non-evidential for the evidential adverbials. This labelling is not as trivial as it may seem at first sight: the difficulties involved in distinguishing epistemic modality from other categories are widely attested in the literature (Simon-Vandenbergen and Aijmer 2007, Nuyts 2005, Collins 2009, Boye and Harder 2009, Cornillie 2009).

In accordance with the definitions of epistemic modality and evidentiality described above, the criteria for their delimitation in this research have to be semantic. For this reason, a preliminary study of the adverbials was carried out, based on the references mentioned above and others (Byloo, Kastein and Nuyts 2007, Maíz and Arús 2008, Tucker 2001, Hoye 1997, Swan 1988). These references attest the importance of pragmatic and discourse factors in global accounts of the adverbials; however, in order to maintain the status of epistemic modality and evidentiality as semantic categories, the decision was made to ignore these factors at this stage of the work. A more detailed account of these pragmatic factors is provided in Carretero and Zamorano-Mansilla (to appear). For the purposes of this paper, suffice it to say that a common feature of these factors is the bleaching of the epistemic or evidential meaning into a more general meaning of modifying assertiveness. On the one hand, epistemic adverbs of probability and possibility, together with the evidential adverbial

[3] Examples of these approaches are Biber et al. (1999) and Kärkkäinen (2003).

[4] Originally, *impossibly* was also listed, but later it was excluded due to the almost total lack of epistemic meaning.

apparently, are often used as downtoners, with the main purpose of expressing a high degree of tentativeness rather than assessing probability. For example, *maybe* in (1) is used to downtone the strength of a suggestion rather than to express an assessment of weak probability:

(1) Every day, I always used to stick my head around the office door and say, 'Anything for me today?' — and one day they said, 'Well, we're looking for dancers for the BBC's production of Pistol Shot (which was a play by Chekhov) — **maybe** you'd like to do it and choreograph it and use some of your students?' (BNC AB5)

On the other hand, epistemic and evidential adverbials of certainty are frequently used with the main purpose of enhancing assertiveness rather than making an assessment of certainty. For example, the main function of *certainly* in (2) is to lay emphasis on the speaker's commitment to comply with the request:

(2) Lord Hulton turned to me. "You'll let us have some more Propopamide, won't you, Herriot?" "**Certainly**," I replied. "I think I have some in the car." (BNC G3S)

It is also well-known that epistemic and evidential adverbials often perform certain discourse functions. The most remarkable of all is, perhaps, the signalling of concessive relationships between the clause in which they occur and another clause. We believe that this discourse function is compatible with the epistemic or evidential meaning: for example, the concessive relationships signalled by *maybe* in (3) and by *certainly* in (4) do not interfere with their respective meanings of possibility and certainty. For this reason, the adverbials were considered as epistemic or evidential in this kind of contexts.

(3) **Maybe** the farmer or his tenant will ask for a percentage of the kill within the agreement, but it makes jolly good sense to ensure that anyone who likes to eat a rabbit and who can influence your sport is well looked after (BNC BNY).

(4) Orcs are bigger than Goblins, more dangerous, and more brutally ambitious.Grom was to prove the exception, a Goblin who was not only as dangerous and ambitious as the best Orc, but vastly bigger as well! It was not that Grom was especially tall, **certainly** not as tall as an Orc, but he was enormously and infamously fat (BNC CMC).

Once the pragmatic factors of modification of assertiveness and concession were identified as distractors, the authors started the annotation task, with the 20 examples of each of the adverbs selected above. The results of the annotation confirmed that a number of semantic factors clearly provoked disagreement. Some of these factors are explained in Section 4.

4 An account of the disagreement-provoking factors

4.1 Generic statements

The adverbials of possibility *conceivably, maybe, perhaps, possibly* and *improbably often occurred* in statements such as (5), which are characterized by the following two features: a) the modalized sentence refers to a class of entities and can therefore be considered as generic, and b) the modal adverbial is paraphraseable by adverbials of frequency such as *sometimes*:

(5) 'Many companies are placing their main focus on the opportunities for intro-European trading after 1992 and rightly so. However, at British Airways Cargo it is the global implications of the Single Market which are receiving most attention,' says Peter White. He continues: Currently, major manufacturers from the United States and Asia tend to have two or **maybe** three plants in Europe.'(BNC AMH)

In these cases, the epistemic adverb may be argued to maintain its epistemic meaning, since there is some probability for the state of affairs to occur in each individual case (that is, whenever there is a major manufacturer from the United States and Asia, there is a possibility that s/he has three plants in Europe). However, the modal adverb could also be considered to express dynamic modality. This modality consists of the set of meanings that belong to the possibility-necessity axis and are determined by natural circumstances, which may or may not be inherent to a person or another entity. The main meanings included in dynamic modality are inevitability, tendency, ability and (lack of) potentiality due to internal properties of an entity or else to circumstantial properties (Zamorano-Mansilla and Carretero to appear). *Maybe* in statements such as (5) is close to dynamic modality, since it describes a tendency of the manufacturers described above.

This semantic complexity accounted for the majority of the cases of disagreement of *possibly* and *conceivably* (these cases are, altogether, 5 for *possibly* and 6 for *conceivably*).[5] Consequently, the decision was made to annotate these occurrences taking into account the overall meanings of the adverbs concerned. The cases of *perhaps* and *maybe* in generic statements were annotated as epistemic, since these adverbs do not display other cases of dynamic modality apart from these; in this way, the adverbs *perhaps* and *maybe* y contrast, *possibly* and *conceivably* have a more established dynamic meaning (Zamorano-Mansilla and Carretero, to appear): in certain cases, as in (6), they are not paraphraseable with *perhaps* or *maybe*. For this reason, the decision was made to annotate their occurrences with generic statements, as in (7), as cases of merger between epistemic and dynamic modality.

(6) In 1939, as in the 1920s, any imports that could **conceivably** be replaced by nationally produced goods had to be reduced to a minimum or stopped. (BNC HPV)

(7) When the radio is switched on, this voltage, stored on C1, is temporarily let loose on the circuitry, where it could **conceivably** do some damage. After a moment, of course, the voltage subsides to its on-load value, which is smaller. (BNC C92)

Generic statements also occurred with *improbably*, concretely with the collocation *however improbably*. The decision was also made to annotate them as cases of merger between epistemic and dynamic modality:

(8) Suppose that, however **improbably**, a balanced slate could nevertheless be agreed on in one party. It is a safe bet that the other parties in contention would not make the same mistake. (BNC EW4)

4.2 Impossibility

Another factor that gave rise to disagreement in the annotation of *possibly* and *conceivably*, and of *plausibly* to a lesser extent, was negative polarity, more specifically the combinations of these adverbials with *cannot* or *could not*. It may well be considered that dynamic impossibility entails epistemic impossibility: a statement that nature does not allow the occurrence of a state of affairs entails that the probabilities for it to occur are none, as in (9), about which the sp/wr has no doubts:

(9) Now you can't **possibly** test a medicine on ten thousand people before you start to sell it, so that sort of risk, as rare a risk as that, will only be picked up when the medicine has actually been in use and on the market and been properly prescribed for some years. (BNC KRE)

However, in other cases impossibility may be indirectly inferred from evidence, and the sp/wr may be interpreted to have a slight doubt (10). Since these cases often led to inter-annotator disagreement, the decision was made to consider them as dynamic, together with the others.

(10) His car was found with bloodstains on the steering-wheel. "He couldn't **possibly** do a thing like that," his best friend said. (BNC H7A)

Other cases of disagreement occurred with the collocation of *only* with *can / could* and *possibly / conceivably*. *Only* has a similar effect to negative polarity ("not... but"), so that the modal meaning of the expressions shifts from weak to strong. These occurrences are annotated as dynamic, in a similar way to the treatment of impossibility described above:

(11) However, Przeworski (1980 and 1985) explores two possible consequences of liberal democracy for the proletariat. First, workers as the majority group in the electorate might rationally choose to maintain capitalism, not because they are duped by the dominant ideology but because their individual interests are better met under redistributive capitalism than through a painful transition to socialism, which could only **conceivably** deliver net benefits in the very long run. (BNC CS3)

4.3 Interrogative structures

The occurrences of the modal adverbials of possibility in interrogative structures were also an area of disagreement. The peculiarities of the use of epistemic expressions in interrogative structures, widely reported in the literature (see, for example, Palmer (1990) and Coates (1983), among others) is due to the fact that questions often implicate the

[5] For *conceivably*, this result corresponds to a second experiment, which had to take place because the annotators realized that both had overused the label 'epistemic' in the first experiment.

sp/wr's lack of total certainty, which coincides with the meaning of epistemic expressions. In fact, these adverbials tend to occur in speculative questions for which the sp/wr does not really expect to get an answer. For instance, (12) could be interpreted as a question about naturally possible reasons (dynamic), or else as epistemic, in the sense that the sp/wr is thinking (in vain) about the correct answer. There is perhaps very little difference between asking about naturally possible reasons and about possibly real reasons. In order to favour inter-annotator agreement, these cases were considered as dynamic.

(12) 'No. Dad gives us money.' Ashamed, she hung her head and scraped a pattern on the dry ground with her toe. 'Then what do you want to get it published for?' 'I don't know.' She looked at him through her lashes, almost sullenly. What other reason could there **possibly** be? 'I just thought people did get books published', she said lamely (BNC HH9)

4.4 Epistemic qualifications whose scope is not exactly that of the clause in which they occur

Some occurrences of the adverb *plausibly* are clearly epistemic (13) and others are clearly non-epistemic, such as (14), in which this adverb refers to the adequacy of a word or expression as a descriptor of an entity or situation:

(13) The larger troops, **plausibly**, were developed as protection from diurnal predators. (BNC AMG)

(14) The novel can **plausibly** be labelled science fiction by virtue of the fact that it takes place in the future and involves' alien' life forms. (BNC G1N)

However, this adverbial displayed a large number of cases of disagreement (9 out of 20), most of which concern the reasonability of a statement made by someone else. The verb often expresses a process of saying (*argue, propose, say, suggest, etc.*). In these cases, the use of *plausibly* means epistemic modality on the part of the sp/wr, but this modality does not affect the proposition in which *plausibly* occurs, but the following proposition (i.e. the proposition expressed by the subordinate clause introduced by the verb of saying). For example, *plausibly* in (15) does not qualify the statement that the suggestion had been made, but the fact that the 'negative' idea was inspired by the custom mentioned there:

(15) The figures are left in the orange colour of the clay, the background painted in round them in the shiny black: a purely decorative variation; and it has been **plausibly** suggested that the strange 'negative' idea was inspired by the custom of washing the background of marble reliefs with a blue or red against which the mainly white figures were left standing out. (BNC FPW)

The decision was made to consider these cases as epistemic, since the modalized proposition is expressed in the same sentence in which *plausibly* occurs.

4.5 Neighbouring epistemic lexical verbs

The occurrence of a modal lexical verb in the clause in which the adverbials occur can bring about additional complexity to the annotation of adverbials of possibility. For example, in (16), *could conceivably* occurs with negative polarity and is therefore to be classified as dynamic; however, the presence of the verb *believe* turned out to be a distractor:

(16) Looking at the matter generally, I can not believe [sic] that that could **conceivably** have been the intention of Parliament when passing the Children Act 1989 (BNC FC0)

Similarly, the occurrence of *believe* seems to have distracted one of the annotators in (17), a case of *plausibly* about the reasonability of a statement made by someone else (see 4.4.) in which the verb expresses a process of thinking and not of saying.

(17) Concurrent with the building of the earliest, a timber grave chamber was constructed beneath its floor to receive the decomposed remains of a middle-aged man. This is **plausibly** believed to be Gorm, Harald's father, originally interred in pagan fashion (BNC HXX)

As a consequence of this distracting effect of verbs such as *believe,* the design of the annotation system could well include specific instructions about the coexistence of the adverbials with *believe* and similar verbs such as *think* or *suppose*, with authentic examples and their correct annotation.

4.6 Gradable adjectives or adverbs

Gradability is a complicating factor that affects the annotation of adverbials of certainty, most of which often occurred with gradable Adjectival Groups or Adverbial Groups under their scope, as in (18-19). In these cases, the adverbials can be roughly paraphrased with intensifiers such as *very*, so that the meanings of certainty and of degree may well be considered to merge. However, a number of dictionaries[6] did not register a meaning of degree in some of the adverbs, such as *decidedly, definitely* and *positively*. Consequently, examples of this kind were annotated as epistemic.

(18) Unfortunately, faced with price increases of up to 25 per cent, many of us decided we could live without champagne. Frankly, it wasn't much of a sacrifice. The sparkling alternatives were getting better and better, thanks largely to the overseas investment of champagne houses, and the basic quality of champagne was **decidedly** dodgy. 1991 levels, but consumers continue to vote with their wallets. (BNC FBL)

(19) They are making a mistake because the Costa Brava has everything anyone could ever want - in large quantities. It is rapidly becoming the playground for some of Europe's most sophisticated and cosmopolitan young people. The French, Italians, Scandinavians, Dutch and Swiss come to play at prices that make some new hot spots look **positively** expensive. (BNC AM0)

4.7 Coexistence of the meanings of certainty and firm decision

The adverbial *definitely* displays clear epistemic cases, roughly paraphraseable with *certainly*, as well as a few non-epistemic cases, which are characterized by the following features: a) paraphraseability of *definitely* by *finally*, while replacement with *certainly* would provoke a semantic change; b) emphasis on the firmness of voluntary decisions; and c) occurrence with processes of saying (*approve, say, state, decide*). An example is (20):

(20) Very few projects are **definitely** approved, with the Space Telescope the major exception. (BNC B7N)

However, other cases of *definitely* are not so clear: they report a firm decision, but at the same time the adverbial may be replaced by *certainly* with little change of meaning (21). In order to achieve a greater degree of agreement, paraphraseability with *certainly* was considered as the key criterion, so that many doubtful cases were subsequently annotated as epistemic.

(21) So you weren't going out with him? "Oh – no. **Definitely** not. It's never a good idea to get too involved with a colleague. (BNC C8D)

4.8 Evidentiality and epistemicity: the case of *apparently*

In the annotation of *apparently*, all the occurrences were unanimously tagged as evidential except for two, one of which is (22). The reason for the disagreement turned out to be that in all the cases except these there was an epistemic implicature that the sp/wr did not know the truth of the proposition. The difference may be seen if we compare (22) with (23): in (22), the Geordies, against appearances, turned out not to be invincible; in (23), the sp/wr implicates that s/he is not absolutely sure that the king repeatedly climbed the town wall.

(22) Keegan, who ten days ago was boss of an **apparently** invincible Geordie side, said: 'I know what people are thinking, but the only difference between our defeat at Leicester on Saturday and our early season results was that we gave away a silly goal.' (BNC CEP)

(23) The king was the guest of Richard Wolph, a prosperous gentleman farmer, until the evening of May 4th, when he left by the same gate for Southwell. **Apparently** he repeatedly climbed the town wall during his stay to watch for his pursuers. (BNC CBB)

The disagreement was due to the error made by one of the annotators of considering the epistemic status of *apparently* for its annotation. However, it was previously agreed that this adverbial is to be annotated in terms of evidentiality and not of epistemic modality. Consequently, it is to be always annotated as evidential: even in cases such

---

[6] The dictionaries consulted were:

- Cambridge Advanced Learner's Dictionary: http://dictionary.cambridge.org/dictionary/british/
- Merriam-Webster Dictionary:
- http://www.merriam-webster.com/dictionary/
- Macmillan English Dictionary for Advanced Learners (2002).

as (22), in which it qualifies a proposition that is not true, it still provides evidence in favour of the hypothetical truth of that proposition. That is to say, its evidential value is constant, while its epistemicity is generated by default, thus having the status of a Generalized Conversational Implicature (Levinson 2000; Carretero 2004); that is to say, *apparently* implicates that the sp/wr does not know the truth or the falsehood of the proposition except when there is contrary evidence to this lack of knowledge.

4.9 Coexistence and pragmatic neutralization of the meanings of evidentiality and manner

The evidential adverbials *clearly* and *plainly* display evidential cases as well as non-evidential cases, which indicate ease of perception (as in 'He spoke clearly'). Only the first kind of cases are paraphraseable by the construction 'it + BE + clear/plain + that'. However, a few occurrences were not readily classifiable, and could even be considered as cases of pragmatic neutralization between the evidential meaning and the meaning of manner. These occurrences did not provoke much disagreement in the annotation (one case of each of *clearly* and *plainly*); however, they did provoke doubtfulness during the annotation process. One of these cases is (24), for which the interpretations "must be set in a clear way…" (manner) and "it is clear that the actualized instances must be set…" (evidential) are both possible: from the pragmatic point of view, there is not much difference between them, since the sp/wr's aims to communicate, above all, that it is necessary to set actualized instances of linguistic signs in correspondence with their conventional meanings:

(24) The conventional meaning of linguistic signs, and their combinations in sentences, constitutes types of conceptualization codified as linguistic knowledge and the tokens of particular and actualized instances must **clearly** be set in correspondence with them. (BNC CBR)

Similarly, in (25), the interpretations "the terms state in a clear way…" (manner) and "it is clear that the terms state…" (evidential) are both possible, and their difference is pragmatically of little importance, the main point being that the terms leave no doubt that the carrier has contractual remedies against a subcontractor.

(25) Therefore, the terms of any subcontract should be very carefully drafted. The terms **plainly** state that the carrier has contractual remedies against a subcontractor (BNC CDP)

In order to annotate examples such as (24) and (25), we have considered that the utterances with *clearly* and *plainly* are roughly paraphraseable by 'it is clear that…' and 'it is plain that…', respectively, although the paraphrase lays emphasis on the evidential meaning and bleaches the meaning of manner. Nevertheless, the possibility of this paraphrase has motivated our decision to annotate these cases as evidential.

5 Conclusions

This paper has described a number of factors that have provoked inter-annotator disagreement in the initial annotation experiments carried out with a number of epistemic and evidential English adverbials. The nature of these factors is diverse: two of them, interrogative structures and clausal scope, could be classified as syntactic, although they need to be explained in terms of the meanings of the structures involved. Other factors concern the meaning of the adverbials themselves in certain contexts, concretely the meanings of impossibility, manner and firm decision, as well as the relationship between evidential and epistemic meanings. Finally, other factors are related to the meaning of the clause in which the adverbials occur (generic statements) or the meanings of other expressions in the surrounding linguistic contexts, such as epistemic lexical verbs or gradable adjectives or adverbs.

In all the cases described here, solutions have been provided for prospective annotation. The application of these solutions (and others to be provided) should result in a high degree of inter-annotator agreement by experts in the second experiment contemplated in the project. The confirmation of this agreement is to be followed by annotation by non-experts. Before embarking on the annotation tasks, these annotators are to receive instructions, which will include these problematic cases and the respective solutions. This procedure should lead to robust annotation systems of epistemic modality and evidentiality that guarantee a high degree of inter-annotator agreement not only among experts, but also among non-experts.

References

Lloyd B. Anderson. 1986. Evidentials, paths of change, and mental maps: Typologically regular asymmetries. In: Wallace Chafe and Johanna Nichols (eds.), Evidentiality: The Linguistic Coding of Epistemology. Ablex, Norwood.

Douglas Biber, Stig Johansson, Geoffrey Leech, Susan Conrad and Edvard Finegan. 1999. Longman grammar of spoken and written English. Longman, London.

Kasper Boye and Peter Harder. 2009. Evidentiality: linguistic categories and grammaticalization. Functions of Language, 16.1: 9-43.

Pieter Byloo, Richard Kastein and Jan Nuyts. 2007. On *certainly* and *zeker*. In: Mike Hannay and Gerard J. Steen (eds.), Structural-functional Studies in English Grammar. John Benjamins, Amsterdam/Philadelphia.

Marta Carretero and Juan Rafael Zamorano-Mansilla. Forthcoming. Disentangling epistemic modality, neighbouring categories and pragmatic uses: The case of English epistemic adverbs. Collection linguistique Épilogos.

Marta Carretero. 2004. Levinson's *Presumptive meanings*: a neo-Gricean approach to pragmatics. In: Marta Carretero, Honesto Herrera-Soler, Gitte Kristiansen and Julia Lavid, (eds.) Estudios de lingüística aplicada a la comunicación. Universidad Complutense, Madrid.

Wallace Chafe. 1986. Evidentiality in English conversation and academic writing. In: Wallace Chafe and Johanna Nichols (eds.), Evidentiality: The Linguistic Coding of Epistemology. Ablex, Norwood.

Jennifer Coates. 1983. The Semantics of the Modal Auxiliaries. Croom Helm, London.

Peter Collins. 2009. Modals and Quasi-modals in English. Rodopi, Amsterdam.

Bert Cornillie. 2009. Evidentiality and epistemic modality: On the close relationship between two different categories. Functions of Language, 16.1: 44-62.

Lars Hermerén. 1978. On Modality in English: the Study of the Semantics of the Modals. Gleerup, Lund.

Leo Francis Hoye. 1997. Modals and Adverbs in English. Longman, London and New York.

Elly Ifantidou. 2001. Evidentials and Relevance. John Benjamins, Amsterdam/Philadelphia.

Elise Kärkkäinen. 2004. Epistemic Stance in English Conversation. John Benjamins, Amsterdam/Philadelphia.

Julia Lavid, Jorge Arús, Juan Rafael Zamorano-Mansilla. 2010. Designing and exploiting a small online English-Spanish parallel corpus for language teaching purposes. In: Mari Carmen Campoy-Cubillo, Begoña Bellés-Fortuño and María Lluïsa Gea-Valor, (eds.) Corpus-based approaches to English Language Teaching. Continuum, London.

Julia Lavid. 2008. CONTRASTES: An Online English-Spanish Textual Database for Contrastive and Translation Learning. In Barbara Lewandowska-Tomaszczyk, (ed.) Corpus Linguistics, Computer Tools, and Applications – State of the Art. Peter Lang, Frankfurt.

Julia Lavid. 2012. Corpus Annotation in CONTRANOT: Linguistic and Methodological Challenges. In: Isabel Moskowitz and Begoña Crespo, (eds.) Encoding the Past: Decoding the Future: Corpora in the 21st Century. Cambridge Scholars Publishing, Newcastle upon Tyne.

Stephen C. Levinson. 2000 Presumptive meanings. The theory of Generalized Conversational Implicature. MIT Press, London, UK and Cambridge, USA.

Carmen Maíz and Jorge Arús. 2008. Towards a diachronic study of modal adverbs: a case study of *certainly*. Philologia, 2008, 27-36.

Marianne Mithun. 1986. Evidential diachrony in Northern Iroquoian. In: Wallace Chafe and Johanna Nichols (eds.), Evidentiality: The Linguistic Coding of Epistemology. Ablex, Norwood.

Jan Nuyts. 2001. Epistemic Modality, Language and Conceptualization: A Cognitive-Pragmatic Perspective. John Benjamins, Amsterdam/Philadelphia.

Jan Nuyts. 2005. The modal confusion: On terminology and the concepts behind it. In: Alex Klinge and Henrik Høeg Müller (eds.), Modality: Studies in Form and Function. Equinox, London.

Frank R. Palmer. 1990 [1979]. Modality and the English Modals. Longman, London and New York.

Michael R. Perkins. 1983. Modal Expressions in English. Frances Pinter, London.

Anne-Marie Simon-Vandenbergen and Karin Aijmer. 2007. The Semantic Field of Modal Certainty. A Corpus-based Study of English Adverbs. Mouton de Gruyter, Berlin and New York.

Toril Swan. 1988. Sentence Adverbials in English: a Synchronic and Diachronic Investigation. Novus Forlag, Oslo.

Gordon Tucker. 2001. Possibly alternative modality. Functions of Language, 8.2, 183-216.

Anna Wärnsby. 2006. (De)coding Modality. The Case of *Must*, *May*, *Måste* and *Kan*. Lund Studies in English 113. Lund University, Lund.

Juan Rafael Zamorano-Mansilla and Carretero, Marta. (in press). An annotation scheme for dynamic modality in English and Spanish. In: Maite Taboada, Susana Doval Suárez and Elsa González Álvarez (eds.) Contrastive discourse analysis: Functional and corpus perspectives. Equinox, London.

Annotating Modal Expressions in the Chinese Treebank

Yanyan Cui **Ting Chi**
Department of Linguistics, Georgetown University
1437 37th Street, NW, Poulton Hall 240
Washington, DC 20057-1051
{yc285, tc374}@georgetown.edu

Abstract

This paper reports an effort to annotate modality in the Penn Chinese Treebank. We introduce the modals and features that were annotated, and describe the phases of our working process. Along with this, we address the issues in the preparation of annotation guidelines, and present the preliminary results of the first pass. Finally, we analyze the types of disagreement, and propose directions to improve consistency.

1 Introduction

Since its release to the public in 2000, the Penn Chinese Treebank (Xia et al.1999) has been annotated with several layers of semantic information such as predicate-argument structures and discourse connectives (Xue 2003, 2005). Our effort, as a part of a larger cross linguistic annotation project, aims to expand this body of work with modal annotation.

Modality is the aspect of meaning that expresses states of affairs beyond the **actual** (Hacquard 2011). Distinguishing between the actual versus modal information is necessary for a wide range of natural language processing (NLP) applications such as sentiment analysis (Wiebe et al. 2005), question answering (Saurí et al 2006), medical information extraction (Mowery et al. 2012), etc.

In recent years, many efforts have been made to create resources of manually annotated modality information. These resources vary greatly in terms of what aspects of modality are annotated and how the features are marked. The diverse goals and backgrounds of the researchers determined this variety of annotation schemes. Hacquard and Wellwood (2012), for example, annotated the interpretation (root vs. epistemic) of modal words in a range of embedded contexts. Their goal is to answer a particular formal semantic question--whether epistemic modals contribute to sentence meaning, and consequently can be embedded in various environments. Mowery et al. (2012) on the other hand, targets a particular practical problem, namely distinguishing negated, affirmed and uncertain information in medical texts. Their project annotated the polarity (positive vs. negative) of sentences, and the degree of certainty (moderate vs. high) associated with a statement. Hendrickx et al. (2012) did yet another type of work, which is motivated from a theoretical perspective, but tries to facilitate potential NLP research as well. Their scheme not only covers more semantic properties of modality (what is the trigger, what is its target, who is the source of the modality, etc.), but also has a more fine-grained distinction of modal values (eight main values and several sub-values).

The goal of our annotation is similar to that of Hendrickx et al. We aim to create a resource that provides detailed semantic analyses to a set of prototypical modal expressions in Mandarin. The produced corpus will allow for both linguistic studies (e.g. the ranges of constructions a certain modal expression occurs) and various machine learning experiments.

A secondary goal of our project is to test the cross-linguistic adaptability of the schema we adopt, which is originally developed by Rubinstein et al. (2013). This schema is supposed to be language-independent, and we applied it to Mandarin with minimum modification.

Started in the fall of 2012, we have so far completed the first pass of annotation on 200 files in the Treebank which are articles from Xinhua newswire[1]. In this process, several goals are achieved:

- We created a first draft of annotation guidelines by modifying the guidelines designed for the parallel English annotation task.
- We calculated agreement measures for different granularities of various annotated features.
- We learned of the difficulties involved in annotation of individual features.

The paper is organized as follows. In section 2, we provide an overview of the project by outlining the modal inventory, the features annotated, and the working process. In section 3, we discuss the issues involved in developing guidelines. Section 4 presents the results of the first pass of annotation, and section 5 discusses the disagreement patterns revealed by these results. Finally, we conclude the paper in section 6.

2 Overview

The annotation is carried out with MMAX2 (Müller & Strube 2006), with a scheme of ten features, and an evolving modal-list. Two annotators are involved, and they are also responsible for the creation of guidelines and quality control.

2.1 Working process

Expecting constant modification of guidelines as well as human errors that need to be corrected regularly, we break the process into small rounds. Each round consists of around 200 files and is divided into four phases, (i) preprocessing of files, (ii) a blind double annotation, (iii) an evaluation, and (iv) a revision. In preprocessing, files to be annotated are prepared, and modals in the modal-list are pre-highlighted for the annotators. In the second phase, the two annotators work independently without discussion. In the next phase, disagreement is measured and analyzed. The inconsistent instances are retrieved and reconsidered. The two annotators work together to resolve the disagreement. In the meantime, guidelines are revised to account for newly encountered issues, while true ambiguities (Rubinstein 2012) will be embraced by keeping both annotations. After revision, the result is re-evaluated then re-revised, until the consistency achieves a pre-decided threshold.

PHASES

Preprocessing
Pre-highlighting modals in the modal-list

Annotation
Blind double annotation: 200 files

Evaluation
Measure Inter-annotator agreement
(using Kappa score)
Analyze disagreement
(employing confusion matrix)

Revision
Correct errors
Resolve disagreement
Revise guidelines

Table 1: working process

2.2 Modal list

The initial modal-list contains 11 entries collected from linguistic literature, most of which are auxiliary verbs. In the first pass, some adverbs are discovered and added to the modal inventory. The updated modal-list is shown in Table 2; the cells containing the acquired modals are shaded.

2.3 Features

Annotators mark not only modality type but also the relation between a modal and various components of the sentence. The annotated features are enumerated in Table 3.

[1] We completed blind double annotation and evaluation, but have not finished error correction and guidelines revision.

Item	Pinyin	POS	Gloss	#token
可能	keneng	Aux.	possible	74
应该	yinggai	Aux.	should	6
会	hui	Aux	sill	40
可	ke	Aux	can/may	39
必须	bixu	Aux	must	12
得	dei	Aux	have to	8
要	yao	Aux	need to	48
可以	keyi	Aux	may	17
能	neng	Aux	be able to	27
能够	nenggo	Aux	be able to	6
一定	yiding	Adv	definitely	3
将	jiang	Adv	will	143
可望	kewang	Adv	hopefully	5
无望	wuwang	Adv	impossible	0
应	ying	Adv	should	4
total				432

Table 2: modal-list

FEATURE	DESCRIPTION
Modality type	The flavor of modals; e.g. *epistemic*, *deontic*, etc
Predicate type	Whether the modal is in its comparative, equative or superlative form
Prejacent	The propositional argument of the modal
Modified element	The NP , AdjP that are modified by the modal
Degree indicator	The element that indicates the degree of the modal
Source	The entity that is responsible for the knowledge, rules etc. that the modal claim is based on; e.g. [$_{source}$John] believes that Mary might come.
Background	Information that provides the background of the modal statement; see(1)
Environmental attitude	The attitude verb embedding the modal; see (1)
Environmental polarity	Whether the modal is in the scope of a sentential negation
Outscoping quantifier	A quantifier in the syntactic scope of a modal but semantically scopes over it

Table 3: features

Priority

- Deontic: the claim is based on rules, standards, social norms, etc.

(1a) *Xinwen bixu zhenshi.*
News must real
'News must be real.'

- Bouletic: the claim is based on desires

(1b) You should try this chocolate[*].

- Teleological: the claim is based on one's goal

(1c) *Zhongguo bixu jinxing gaige, yi zengqiang*
China must make reform to improve
zishen jingzhengli.
self competitiveness
'China must make reforms to improve its competitiveness.'

Dynamic (ability_circumstantial)

- Circumstantial: the claim is based on circumstances

(1d) *Zai ci jichu shang, jinnian de jingji*
prep. this basis *loc.* this year DE. economy
zengzhang mubiao wanquan keyi shixian.
growth goal completely can realize
'On this basis, this year's goal of economic growth can absolutely be achieved.'

- Ability: the claim is based on what the agent can do

(1e) *Zhongguo yi neng shengchan shang wan men*
China already can produce over 10,000 Cl.
shuzi dianhua chengkong jiaohuanji
digital telephone SPC exchange
'China can already produce over 10,000 digital telephone SPC exchanges.'

Epistemic

- the claim is based on's belief of knowledge

(1f) *Jingguo shidang tiaozheng, dongya jingji*
through proper adjustments East Asia economy
yiding hui jixu xiangqian fazhan
definitely will continue forward develop
'With proper adjustment, the economy of East Asia will continue to develop.'

Table 4: examples of modality types

Following the hierarchical classification of modal flavors proposed by Portner (2009), we consider six atomic values for modality type:

[*] We have not encountered any instance both annotators mark as bouletic. The example is from Portner (2009), p133.

epistemic, circumstantial, ability, deontic, bouletic and teleological. The last three values are subtypes of **priority** modal, while circumstantial and ability are subtypes of **dynamic** modal*. In cases where fine-grained decisions cannot be made, coarser categories are available for selection. For priority modals, in addition to the super-type *priority*, there is an option bouletic_teleological. For non-priority modals, there are epistemic_circumstantial and ability_circumstantial. These collapsed values are created on the basis of a pilot study run on Amazon's Mechanical Turk. (Rubinstein et al 2012).

Table 4 provides descriptions and examples for the atomic values; instances of the coarse classes are shown in (2a-c):

<u>bouletic_teleological</u>

(2a) *Su-gang yao kao da yunhe*
Su-gang need to rely on great canal
yunshu yuanliao he chengpin
transport raw material and product
'Su-gang Group needs to transport raw materials and products via the Great Canal.'

<u>epistemic_circumstantial</u>

(2b) *Shenzhen tequ jinnian guonei*
Shenzhen special district this year domestic
shengchan zongzhi ke da yiqianyibaisanshiyi
product gross can reach 11.3 billion
'GDP of Shenzhen this year can reach 11.3 billion (yuan).'

<u>ability_circumstantial</u>

(2c) *Wanqi yi-gan jibing wangwang hui*
advanced hepatitis B disease often can
zhuanhua wei ai
turn to as cancer
'Advanced stage of hepatitis B can often turn to cancer.'

Modal tokens rarely appear with all ten features. At minimum, *modality type* is specified for each modal, and in most cases, the *prejacent* of modals is marked as well. Other frequent features include *background* and *environmental attitude*. (3) illustrates how these features are annotated.

* The term *dynamic* is not used in the schema. Instead the combination ability_circumstantial is adopted.

(3) *Ju shanghai shi ji-wei*
according to Shanghai-city planning committee
zhuanjia ***[fenxi yuce***], [*yao zai 2000*
expert analyze estimate want to in 2000
nian shixian ren-jun guonei shengchan
year realize per capita domestic product
zong-zhi wu qian meiyuan de mubiao,]
gross five thousand dollar DE goal
[*jin-hou san nian hanghai guonei*
from now three year Shanghai domestic
shengchan zong-zhi pingjun nian-zengfu]
product gross average annual-growth
yao[teleological] [*dadao bai-fen-zhi-shi zhi*
need to arrive at 10% to]
bai-fen-zhi-yi
eleven percent

'According to the analysis and estimation by the experts from the planning committee of Shanghai city, to achieve a per capita GDP of five thousand dollars by the year 2000 in the following three years, the annual GDP growth of Shanghai needs to be around 10% to 11%. '

- **modal**: yao, 'need to'
- **modality type**: priority --> teleological
- **prejacent**: 'in the following three years, the annual GDP growth of Shanghai needs to be around 10% to 11%'
- **background**: 'to achieve a GDP of five thousand dollars by the year 2000'
- **environmental attitude**: 'analyze and estimate'

3 Development of Guidelines

Because this effort is part of a larger cross linguistic annotation, in order to maintain consistency with the other project, we started by applying the guidelines that were originally created for English annotations to the Chinese annotation. It worked well for purely semantic features such as modality type and environmental polarity, but difficulties arise when it comes to the features within the syntax-semantics interface such as span of prejacent.

In cases where no instructions are applicable, we added new specifications. In updating the guidelines, real examples are always included along with the rules. In what follows, we provide examples of the problems we have encountered and the treatments proposed.

Modals with A-not-A forms: In Chinese, a polarity question can be formed by alternating the main predicate of a sentence with its positive form (full form or the first syllable only) followed by its negative form. This kind of question is called an A-not-A question, and the form of the predicate is A-not-A form (Huang et al. 2009). Take (4) for example:

(4) *Qingshaonian* *ke-bu-keyi* *xiyan*
juvenile may-not-may smoke
'May juveniles smoke or not? '

There are two possible annotations for A-not-A forms. One way is to treat an A-not-A form as one modal. The problem of this proposal is that if it is one markable, then the polarity of then sentence will be neither negative nor positive, and thus is illogical. The other solution is to divide A-not-A into two independent modals. The drawback of this approach is redundancy. Since the positive and negative modal will share the same set of features, the annotation is doubled.

After evaluating both approaches, we adopt the first, i.e. A-not-A is one modal, with a minor modification of the scheme, namely, adding a new value, A-not-A, to the *polarity* feature.

Potential complement: Potential complement construction is marked by the particle *de* (得), which appears "inside the so-called verb-result construction (*dongjie shi*) or verb-direction construction (*dongqu shi*)". This construction "has a modal interpretation" (Xie 2012). The negation of a potential complement is formed by replacing *de* with the negation word *bu* (不). Compare (5) and (6):

(5) *Zhangsan ban de qilai na xiang shu*[1]
Zhangsan lift DE up that box(CL) book
'Zhangsan can lift up the box of books.'

(6) *Zhangsan ban bu qilai na xiang shu*
Zhangsan lift not up that box(CL) book
'Zhangsan cannot lift up the box of books.'

Because the modal interpretation contributes to the whole construction rather than to individual components, we treat the whole form "verb *de/bu* complement" as the modal that needs to be annotated. *Bu* is also marked as the item indicating the negative polarity of the sentence.

Relative clauses: The original guidelines for annotating modals in relative clauses specify that the relativizer should be included in the prejacent of the modal; the head noun that the relative clause modifies should not. Consider (7):

(7) The person [*that we* might *see*] is John.

Relative clauses have a different structure in Chinese. They precede the head noun, and do not have a relativizer. Instead, there is a structural particle *de* which connects the relative clause to the nominal head.

We decided to exclude the particle *de* from the span of the prejacent, since it is not a part of the relative clause both syntactically and semantically. See (8):

(8) *Gongsi jueding jiang ke [yingli baiwan*
company decide *prep.* can profit million
yuan yishang] de yi zheng tao ruanjian dui
yuan above DE one whole set software to
yonghu kaifang.
users open

'The company decided to make open-source the whole set of software which can earn a profit of more than one million yuan.'

Temporal phrases: In many cases, a temporal phrase is contained in the syntactic scope of a modal's prejacent. Take (9) as an illustration:

(9) [*Shanghai jin-nian quan nian chukou*] *keyi*
shanghai this year all year export may
[*chaoguo yi bai sis hi wu yi meiyuan.*]
exceed 14.5 billion dollar

'This year, the annual export of Shanghai may exceed 14.5 billion dollars.'

When marking the prejacent, we do not separate temporal phrases, whether they are inside or outside the scope of the modal. The reason for this is because singling out temporal phrases will make the prejacent more fragmented than necessary..

***You* (有)-X-modal-Y construction:** As illustrated in (10), the modal-Y part expresses certain properties of X, and the verb *you* 'have'

[1]The example is modified form Xie (2012), (1).

expresses the existence of X. For example, in *you-fa-ke-yi*, *ke-yi* 'can-abide' modifies the preceding noun *fa* 'law'; and the whole phrase means 'to have laws to abide by'. We did not annotate the modals in this construction, because there is no settled view about its syntactic analysis: It could be a productive morphological template, or it could be a case of postposed relative clause.

(10) a. *shi women [you fa ke yi]*
make we have law can abide
'to make us have laws that we can abide by (have laws to abide by)'

b. *Ta jintian [you gongzuo yao zuo]*
he today have work need to do
'He has work that he needs to do today.'

4 Results

As described in 2.1, we will have multiple cycles of evaluation and revision to control the quality of the annotation. This section presents the result of the first round of evaluation.

4.1 Measures of agreement

We calculated inter-annotator agreement on four features: *modality type*, *prejacent*, *background*, and *degree modifier*. Other features will be evaluated the next step. Two measures, κ score (Cohen 1960) and percentage of agreed instances, are provided. Also note that the annotated instances vary across features.

FEATURE	% OF AGREED	κ	ANNOTATED INSTANCES*
Modality type	62.3	0.522	406 (253)
Degree modifier	97.8	0.390	12 (3)
Background	84.7	0.349	86 (24)
Prejacent	66.5	N/A	406 (270)

Table 5: agreement: multiple features

We set a minimum threshold of 0.6 (Carletta 1996) for kappa scores for the purpose of quality control. As shown in Table 3, the kappa scores are all lower than the threshold. It indicates that all the four features are hard to annotate, and validates the necessity of cyclic evaluation followed by revision.

*The figures in the parentheses are the number of instances annotated by both annotators.

Table 4 provides kappa scores on the agreement of modality type. It presents them before and after category collapsing per individual modal. Possible values of modality type are listed in Table 5.

Modal	κ *all Cat.*	κ *Collapsed*	*#Tokens*
dei	1.0	1.0	8
jiang	0.814	0.852	143
bixu	0.406	1.0	12
neng	0.352	0.632	27
hui	0.322	0.399	40
keneng	0.310	1.0	74
ke	0.283	0.633	39
nenggou	0.28	1.0	8
keyi	0.239	0.443	17
yao	0.099	0.289	48
yinggai	-0.256	1.0	6
overall	0.522	0.815	406

Table 6: agreement: modality type

COLLAPSED	ALL CATEGOREIS
priority	priority(p),deontic(d),bouletic(b), bouletic_teleological(b/t)
non-priority	epistemic(e), circumstantial(c), ability(a), ability_circumstantial(a/c), epistemic_circumstantial(a/c),
not set	not_set (n)
to be decided	to_be_decided (tbd)

Table 7: values and labels of modality types

The agreement scores before collapsing modality types is relatively low for most of the modals. The majority of the scores cluster around 0.3, while the extreme scores (=1.0 or < 0) are attested with low-occurrence modals. The kappa scores are generally improved after collapsing. However, some scores are still below the 0.6 threshold. We will discuss these cases in section 5.

Table 8 is the confusion matrix for modality type as marked by both annotators. We point out two obvious differences between Annotator A (columns) and Annotator B (rows):

- Among the priority types, Annotator A prefers *deontic* over *teleological* (64:13), while Annotator B does not have a strong preference (34:30) between them.

- Annotator A selects the coarse type *epistemic_circumstantial* much more often than Annotator B (31 vs. 3). In cases where the *epistemic_circumstantial* is chosen by Annotator A, Annotator B tended to mark the type as *circumstantial* (23/31).

	e	a	c	e/c	a/c	d	b	t	b/t	p	n	tbd	**S**
e	5	0	5	3	0	0	0	0	0	0	1	0	14
a	1	9	0	0	2	0	0	0	0	0	0	0	12
c	6	1	89	23	8	3	0	0	0	0	4	0	134
e/c	0	0	0	1	1	0	0	0	0	0	1	0	**3**
a/c	0	10	3	3	10	1	0	0	0	0	0	0	27
d	0	0	2	0	0	31	0	1	0	0	0	0	**34**
b	0	0	0	0	0	0	0	0	0	0	0	0	0
t	0	0	0	0	0	16	1	3	9	0	1	0	**30**
b/t	0	0	0	0	0	3	0	5	1	0	1	0	10
p	0	0	0	0	0	2	0	2	0	0	1	0	5
n	0	2	18	1	2	8	0	2	0	0	104	0	137
tbd	0	0	0	0	0	0	0	0	0	0	0	0	0
S	12	22	117	**31**	23	**64**	1	**13**	10	0	113	0	**406**

Table 8: confusion matrix of modality type

5 Discussions

To better understand annotator disagreement, we retrieved the full list of sentences where any of the four features evaluated did not agree among the annotators. Roughly, these instances fall into four classes in terms of the reason for disagreement:

a) *Human error*: Some features are accidentally overlooked by one of the annotators, yielding disagreement.

b) *Vague guidelines*: Lack of specification in the guidelines causes divergent annotations. The low κ of the degree modifier feature can mainly be attributed to vagueness.

c) *Annotator's deviation from guidelines*: Annotators do not always correctly remember the individual instructions in the guidelines, and thus do not always follow them. This type of disagreement is commonly found in the annotation of background and prejacent.

d) *High ambiguity of the target word*: we pointed out in the previous section that even with collapsed modality type, the κ scores of some modals are still relatively low. This is because they have a broader spectrum of meaning.

M	*non-priority*					*non-priority*					n	**K**
	e	a	c	e/c	a/c	d	b	t	b/t	p		
yao												.29 .10
hui												.40 .32
keyi												.44 .24
neng												.63 .35
ke												.63 .28
jiang												.85 .81
ying gai												1.0 -.3
yiding												1.0 -.2
neng gou												1.0 .28
ke neng												1.0 .31
bixu												1.0 .41
dei												1.0 1.0
ke wang												1.0 1.0

Table 9: semantic spectrums of modal inventory

.

Table 9 shows the distribution of modality types annotated for each expression. The cell is shaded if the corresponding type is chosen by at least one annotator. The darker grey cells are the majority types preferred by each annotator. In some cases the types preferred by the two annotators overlap, but mostly they do not. From Table 9 we can generalize:

a). It is more difficult to achieve high agreement on the annotation of a modal's flavor when the modal has many possible interpretations. This coincides with naïve intuitions.

b). If an item has both modal and non-modal usages (*yao, hui, jiang, ke, neng*), then it is likely that the annotation of the item will arrive at a low kappa score.

Take *yao* and *hui* for illustration. These two words have both a modal usage and some other usages. The word *yao* can be used as an attitude verb meaning 'want to'. Similarly, *hui* can be used as a pure future marker without any obvious modal content. (11a-b) provides cases where one of the annotators marked the modality type of the target as *not_set*, i.e. not a modal expression. Table 10 summarizes how often the two tokens are marked as non-modal by each annotator.

(11a) *Oumeng biaoshi yao jinyibu cujin*
E.U. express YAO further promote
shuangfang zai gelingyu de jiaoliu
both parties in each area DE communication
(i) 'EU says that (it) is willing to further promote the communication between the two parties in various areas.'
(ii) 'EU says that the two parties need to further promote their communication in various areas.'

(11b) *Ji nian nei, Xianggang hui chuxian*
several year within, Hong Kong HUI appear
geng-duo de Zhongguo jijin
more DE China fund
(i) 'There will be more funds from China in Hong Kong within several years.'
(ii) 'There can be more funds from China in Hong Kong within several years.'

	Non-modal meaning	# not_set by both	# not_set by A	# not_set by B
yao	'want to'	4	7	12
hui	future marker	8	8	20

Table 10: tokens marked as *not_set*

The effect of modal/non-modal distinction seems to be more significant than the distinction between different flavors of modality. Yet this observation needs to be tested with a larger data set.

6 Conclusion

In this paper, we described our effort to annotate various aspects of modals in Penn Chinese Treebank, and reported the preliminary results of the first pass of annotation. The results show that it is hard for two annotators to achieve high agreement not only for modality type, but also for prejacent, background, and degree modifier. Therefore, multiple cycles of evaluation and revision are necessary for quality control. In effect, our project shows that, with minor adjustments, it is possible to use one scheme and set of guidelines for cross-linguistic annotation.

References

Carletta, J. 1996. Squibs and Discussions Assessing Agreement on Classification Tasks: The Kappa Statistic. *Computational Linguistics*, 22(2), 249-254.

Cohen, J. 1960. A coefficient of agreement for nominal scales. *Educational and Psychological Measurement* 20 (1): 37–46.

Hacquard, V. 2011. Modality in *Semantics: An International Handbook of Natural Language Meaning*. HSK 33.2 ed. C. Maienborn, K. von Heusinger and P. Portner, 1484-1515. Berlin: Mouton de Gruyter.

Hacquard, V. and Wellwood, A. 2012. Embedding epistemic modals in English: A corpus- based study. *Semantics and Pragmatics* 5:1-29.

Hendrickx, I.; Mendes, A.; and Mencarelli, S. 2012. Modality in text: A proposal for corpus annotation. In *Proceedings of the Eight International Conference on Language Resources and Evaluation (LREC'12).*

Huang, C-T. J.; Li, Y-H. A.; and Li, Y. 2009. *The Syntax of Chinese*. Cambridge University Press.

Kratzer, A. 1981. The notional category of modality. In In *Words, worlds, and contexts*, ed. H.-J. Eikmeyer, H. Rieser, 38-74. Walter de Gruyter.

Müller, C.; and Strube, M. 2006. Multi-level annotation of linguistic data with MMAX2. *Corpus technology and language pedagogy*: *New resources, new tools, new method,* ed. S. Braun, K. Kohn, J. Mukherjee, 197-214. Peter Lang.

Portner, P. 2009. *Modality*. Oxford University Press.

Rubinstein, A.; Simonson, D.; Chung, J.; Harner, H.; Katz, G.; and Portner, P. 2012. Developing a methodology for modality type annotations on a large scale. Slides of talk presented at the Modality Workshop, Ottawa University, April.

Rubinstein, A.; Harner, H.; Krawczyk, E.; Simonson, D.; Katz, G.; and Portner, P. 2013. Toward Fine-grained Annotation of Modality in Text. In *Proceedings of the Tenth International Conference for Computational Semantics (IWCS 2013).*

Saurí, R.; Verhagen, M.; and Pustejovsky, J. 2006. Annotating and recognizing event modality in text. In *19th International FLAIRS conference (FLAIRS 2006).*

Wiebe, J.; Wilson, T.; and Cardie, C. 2005. Annotating expressions of opinions and emotions in language. *Language Resources and Evaluation*, 37(2-3):165-210.

Xia, F.; Palmer, M.; Xue, N.; Okurowski, M. E.; Kovarik, J.; Chiou, F. D.; and Marcus, M. 2000. Developing guidelines and ensuring consistency for Chinese text annotation. In *Proceedings of the 2nd International Conference on Language Resources and Evaluation (LREC-2000).*

Xie, Z. 2012. The modal uses of de and temporal shifting in Mandarin Chinese. *Journal of East Asian Linguistics* 21:387-420.

Xue, N. and Palmer, M. 2003. Annotating the propositions in the Penn Chinese Treebank. In *Proceedings of the second SIGHAN workshop on Chinese language processing*. Volume 17 (pp. 47-54).

Xue, N. 2005. Annotating discourse connectives in the chinese treebank. In *Proceedings of the Workshop on Frontiers in Corpus Annotations II: Pie in the Sky* (pp. 84-91).

Influence of modality markers on the conditional interpretation of the German preposition *ohne*

Claudia Roch
Department of Linguistics
Ruhr-Universität Bochum
Bochum, Germany
roch@linguistics.rub.de

Abstract

This paper investigates the impact of modality markers on the conditional interpretation of the German preposition *ohne* ('without'). It tackles the question whether it is the preposition itself that possesses a conditional sense or whether it may be due to a modal context that the interpretation arises. The paper presents an annotation study for modality factors (e.g. mood, modal auxiliary verbs, modal adjectives, modal adverbs, modal infinitives, negation) in the context of these sentences. The statistical analysis of the data has been carried out by means of a correspondence analysis in order to identify the relevant factors for the conditional interpretation. The results suggest that primarily the verb mood has an influence.

1 Conditional interpretation of *ohne*

Conditionality can be expressed by a variety of linguistic means. The most typical form is the conditional sentence that is signaled by the subordinators *if... then...* and establishes a relation between a condition in the antecedent and a depending state of affairs in the consequent. The conditional relation belongs to a subgroup of CCC relations, as they are sometimes referred to (Kortmann, 1997), standing for conditionals, causals, and concessives. But although conditionality is an attested interclausal relation, there are examples in which the same relation is expressed by prepositional phrases, e.g. (1).

(1) *Ohne größere Wanderung ist es kaum*
Without bigger hike is it hardly
möglich die Insel kennenzulernen.
possible the island to.get.to.know
'Without a long hike it is almost impossible to get to know the island.'

The paraphrase of (1) as a conditional sentence stresses the conditional relation: "*If there is no long hike, it is almost impossible to get to know the island.*" In the paraphrase the subordinated *if*-clause expresses the condition in the antecedent, while the matrix clause expresses the depending state of affairs in the consequent. As the preposition *ohne* carries an inherent negation, the negation become explicit in the paraphrase with the *if*-clause. In the former example (1) solely the *ohne*-PP constitutes the antecedent and expresses the condition, which is precisely a negative condition. Negative condition is defined by Kortmann (1997:86) as "*If not p, q: The coming of about q depends on the nonfulfillment of p.*"

But should the preposition *ohne* ('without') hence be attributed a negative conditional interpretation? The preposition *ohne* expresses that something is lacking or absent in general. The set of all senses and subsenses (which are indicated by the underscore) for German *ohne* can be found in Table 1 (cf. Müller and Roch, 2012). Examples are provided in English.

meaning	example
absence	He likes the house without a garden.
modal	
_instrument	He opened the door without a key.
_manner	He walked all the way without shoes.
participation	
_comitative	He went home without his brother.
restrictive	He paid 200 $ without the taxes.
statement	He must be at home without doubt.
governed	He can do without water a few days.

Table 1: Prepositional meanings of *ohne*/'without'

From the lexical resources of German it is reasonable to assume a conditional interpretation. The dictionary of Kempcke (2000) and the dictionary of prepositions by Schröder (1986) list conditional interpretations for *ohne*. But I will argue that there are actually four different interpretations in the class of CCC relations possible for *ohne*. The interpretations are exemplified in Table 2 with examples from English. The examples are relatively similar, because only minor changes in mood and tense of the verb or the addition of an adverb is required in order to arrive at one of the other interpretations within this subclass.

CCC meaning	example
conditional	Without a hike it is impossible to get to know the island.
causal	Without the hike (which was cancelled) we did not get to know the island.
concessive	Even without the hike (which was cancelled) we got to know the island.
conditional-concessive	Even without a hike it is possible to get to know the island.

Table 2: CCC relations of *ohne*/ 'without'

Nevertheless, one has to ask what the semantic contribution of the preposition is. There are three hypotheses available. First, one could suppose that *ohne* possesses a conditional aspect of meaning which goes in accordance with the dictionaries. Secondly, it would also be possible that the preposition has one of its typical other interpretations like 'privation' or 'negation'. Third option is that *ohne* does not carry any meaning at all in these sentences and is semantically vacuous.

For the German preposition *bei*, Grabski and Stede (2006) assume that instead of showing a conditional interpretation, the preposition is left lexically underspecified. According to them the conditional relation is only interpreted by the speaker. It is a slightly different case with *ohne*, as it adds at least the negation.

Clearly, if the second or third option pertains, we have to ask how the conditional interpretation arises in the first place. A possible solution would be to assume that conditionality arises from other factors in the clause, either lexical or constructional. If this solution is viable, the conditional interpretation of *ohne* could be regarded as a pseudo interpretation instead of listing it as one of the senses of the preposition.

2 Modality markers in context

In connection with these considerations we can crucially observe that the conditional interpretation is mostly accompanied by a modal sentence context. One can observe a wide range of modality markers as e.g. subjunctive mood, modal auxiliary verbs, modal adjectives, modal adverbs, the modal infinitive etc. All these modality markers have of course an influence on the factual status of a sentence as they leave it open whether some statement is or becomes a fact in the world. The negation also occurs quite frequently in the context of these sentences. It is an important factor as well as it changes the validity of a statement. Apart from that generic readings are also frequent and must be taken into account. The following examples for the conditional interpretation of *ohne* shall exemplify the prominence of modality contexts.

(2) *Ohne technische Kenntnisse*
Without technical knowledge
kann man das nicht reparieren.
can.MODAUX one this not.NEG repair
'Without technical knowledge one cannot repair it.'

(3) *Er hätte vielleicht*
He have.SBJV maybe.MODADV
ohne Fehlurteil eines Kampfrichters
without misjudgment of.a referee
seinen ersten Sieg erreichen können.
his first victory achieve can.MODAUX
'Without the misjudgment of a referee he maybe could have achieved his first victory.'

In example (2) modality markers are the modal auxiliary verb *können* ('can'), and a negation. The sentence also exhibits a generic interpretation which is indicated by the German pronoun *man* ('one'). Modality is signaled in example (3) by the subjunctive mood in the verb (German *Konjunktiv II*), by the modal adverb *vielleicht* ('maybe') and the modal auxiliary verb *können* again. The occurrences of modality markers and negation etc. are noticeable in the examples. It stands to question what their influence is and whether they may establish the conditional interpretation. The aim of the paper for the moment is to identify the influencing modal factors of the interpretation. The explanation of the data is left for future work.

3 Annotation of modality factors

In order to shed some light on these questions we present a corpus study, which investigates the influence of modality markers on the conditional interpretation. Annotation has been carried out manually for 1332 sentences with an *ohne*-PP. The data set is a part of the NZZ (Neue Zürcher Zeitung) newspaper corpus and already contained annotations for preposition meanings of *ohne* provided in the Bochum preposition project[1]. Table 3 gives the exact numbers of the preposition meaning distribution in the data sample[2].

preposition meaning	number of sentences
1_participation	51
2_causal	28
3_conditional	514
4_conditional_concessive	67
5_concessive	66
6_modal	308
7_governed	8
8_restrictive	9
9_absence	280
10_statement	1

Table 3: Distribution of preposition meanings

[1] http://www.linguistics.rub.de/~kiss/dfg_projekt.html

[2] The meaning '10_statement' does not appear in the analysis, as it has too few instances and was excluded during aggregation. The subsenses exemplified in Table 1 are not distinguished as they are not relevant for the task at hand. The sample is not balanced, but results have proven to be stable with 2000 sentences. As the annotation of the whole dataset of 4216 sentences is not complete the findings must be considered preliminary.

The following list contains the relevant factors for the annotation and the respective values that can be chosen inside a category. The category 'mood_tense' is a combination of the German mood (indicative, imperative, conjunctive I, conjunctive II (subjunctive)) and tense form of the verb (present, preterite, perfect, pluperfect, future I and future II, including infinitives that have no tense). The values for 'mood_tense' can become 'no' if there is no verb available in the sentence. The category 'modal_marker' is also in need of explanation. It subsumes the different markers modal auxiliary verb, modal adjective, modal adverb, and modal infinitive. It becomes 'mod' as soon as one of the modality markers is present, else it must be 'no_mod'.

- mood_tense: {Ind, Imp, KonI/II, no_Pres, Pret, Perf, Plu, FutI/II, Inf, no}
- negation: {neg, no_neg}
- modal_marker: {mod, no_mod}

  ('mod' if modal auxiliary verb, or modal adjective, or modal adverb, or modal infinitive = yes, else 'no_mod')
- generic_specific_reading: {gen, spec}

An annotation example for the modality factors is presented in (5). The annotations belong to the sentence in (1) which is repeated once again in (4):

(4) *Ohne größere Wanderung ist es kaum*
Without bigger hike is it hardly.NEG
möglich die Insel kennenzulernen.
possible.MODADJ the island to.get.to.know
'Without a long hike it is almost impossible to get to know the island.'

(5) Annotations for example (4)
- mood_tense (*ist*): Ind_Pres
- negation (*kaum*): neg
- modal_marker (*möglich*): mod (modal adjective = yes)
- generic_specific_reading: gen

4 Correspondence Analysis (CA)

Correspondence analysis (*CA*, Benzécri, 1973; Clausen, 1998) has been chosen for the statistical analysis. It is a method of multivariate statistics and is suitable to handle categorical variables, like those introduced in (5). Correspondence analysis produces a low-dimensional map in which associations between variables become visible. There are several implementations of correspondence analysis in the R environment available, e.g. in the *ca* package by Nenadić and Greenacre (2007) or in the *languageR* package by Baayen (2008) via the function *corres.fnc*.

As the standard input format correspondence analysis takes a cross tabulation. In the present case it is a cross tabulation of the variable 'preposition meaning' and an interactive variable[3] of all annotated factors. The interactive variable combines the annotations in one large variable of the general form 'mood_tense.negation.modal_marker.generic_specific_reading'. The aim of the analysis is to reveal the hidden associations between the variables. The focus is of course on the conditional interpretation, and whether there are associations with the annotated modality markers.

Table 4 contains the principal inertias and a scree plot (obtained from the *ca* package) for the data. Inertia must be understood as variance. The values indicate how well a dimension explains the variation in the distances between categories in the map. The scree plot is a test that can be used to obtain the appropriate number of dimensions. It means that all dimensions before a clear break in the plot are considered relevant.

Principal inertias (eigenvalues):				
dim	value	%	cum%	scree plot
1	0.450588	47.9	47.9	************************
2	0.152640	16.2	64.1	********
3	0.117962	12.5	76.7	******
4	0.077014	8.2	84.9	***
5	0.060756	6.5	91.3	***
6	0.043893	4.7	96.0	**
7	0.020953	2.2	98.2	
8	0.016715	1.8	100.0	
Total	0.940503	100.0		

Table 4: Principal inertias (eigenvalues) of CA

[3] Cf. Clausen, 1998 for the term 'interactive variable'.

So due to this plot we should definitely include the first three dimensions in the analysis.

In the resulting map of correspondence analysis in Figure 1 the black labels represent the prepositional meanings (cf. Table 3) while the grey labels display the annotated combined modality factors. What immediately catches the eye is that Figure 1 shows a clear separation between the conditional interpretation and the other interpretations of *ohne* on the first axis. The interpretation of the map yields two important observations. The mood feature 'subjunctive' (German *Konjunktiv II*) is grouped in the map together with the conditional interpretation. It appears only in the positive space of the first axis. One can also say that these categories "correspond in space", so we can assume that these variables are associated. Second observation is that the feature 'no_negation' is found in the map in a group with all the other interpretations of *ohne*. The opposite feature 'negation' occurs with the other interpretations only in a few exceptions. In the same area with the conditional interpretation, however, we find both values for negation, so negation is not required for a conditional interpretation, but it occurs quite seldom with the other interpretations of *ohne*. The features 'modality_marker' and 'generic_specific_reading' cannot clearly be set aside in the map, so it must be left open, whether these factors have any influence on the conditional interpretation. The correspondence analysis in the present case cannot explain the influence of these variables.

5 Conclusion

Correspondence analysis has proven a useful method to make associations between categorical variables visible. For the conditional interpretation of the preposition *ohne* it could be shown that there is a considerable influence of the subjunctive mood of the verb. Future studies with more data and reassessment of the factors will maybe reveal more insights into how the conditional interpretation arises.

Acknowledgments

The ideas presented in this paper have benefitted from discussions with Tibor Kiss and the helpful suggestions of three anonymous reviewers whom I would like to thank.

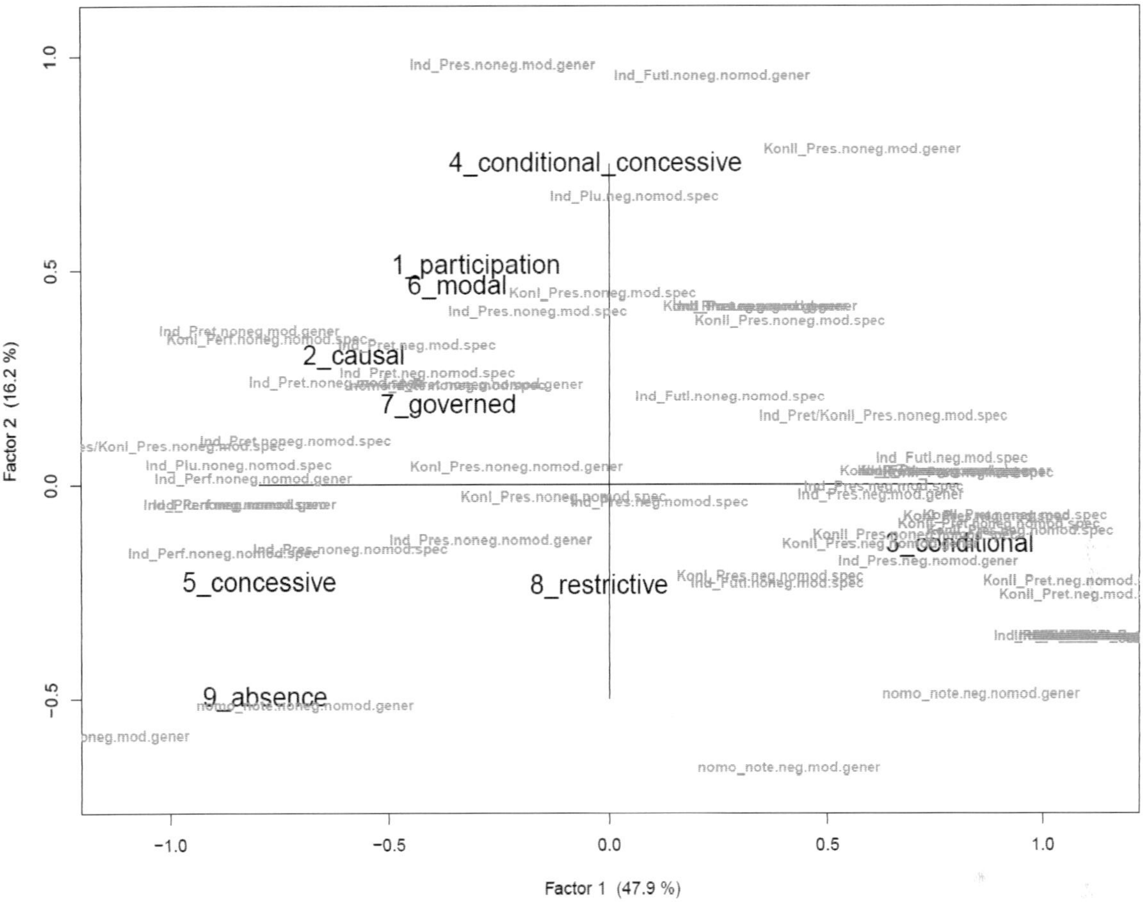

Figure 1: First two dimensions of CA

References

Harald Baayen. 2008. *Analyzing Linguistic Data. A Practical Introduction to Statistics Using R*. Cambridge University Press, Cambridge.

Jean-Paul Benzécri. 1973. *L'analyse des données. Volume II. L'analyse des correspondances*. Dunod, Paris.

Sten-Erik Clausen. 1998. *Applied Correspondence Analysis. An Introduction*. Quantitative Applications in the Social Sciences, 121. Sage Publications, Thousand Oaks, CA.

Michael Grabski and Manfred Stede. 2006. "Bei": Intraclausal Coherence Relations Illustrated With a German Preposition. *Discourse Processes* 41(2).

Günter Kempcke. 2000. *Wörterbuch Deutsch als Fremdsprache*. De Gruyter, Berlin.

Bernd Kortmann. 1997. *Adverbial Subordination: A Typology and History of Adverbial Subordinators Based on European Languages*. De Gruyter, Berlin/New York.

Antje Müller and Claudia Roch. 2012. Präpositionsannotation – Manual. Bochum, Ms.

Oleg Nenadić and Michael Greenacre. 2007. Correspondence Analysis in R, with Two- and Three-dimensional Graphics: The ca Package. *Journal of Statistical Software* 20(3).

Jochen Schröder. 1986. *Lexikon deutscher Präpositionen*. VEB Verlag Enzyklopädie, Leipzig.

Toward Fine-grained Annotation of Modality in Text

Aynat Rubinstein, Hillary Harner, Elizabeth Krawczyk, Daniel Simonson, Graham Katz[†], and Paul Portner

Department of Linguistics
Georgetown University, Washington, DC

{ar1029,hjh34,eak49,des62,portnerp}@georgetown.edu

[†]ekatz@caci.com

Abstract

We present a linguistically-informed schema for annotating modal expressions and describe its application to a subset of the MPQA corpus of English texts (Wiebe et al. 2005). The annotation is fine-grained in two respects: (i) in the range of expressions that are defined as modal targets and (ii) in the amount of information that is annotated for each target expression. We use inter-annotator reliability results to support a two-way distinction between priority and non-priority modality types.

1 Introduction

An important part of understanding natural language depends on the ability to tease apart information about the **actual** from that about the **modal**. From the perspective of textual entailment, for example, a non-modal statement like *The butler is the culprit* supports inferences about the actual state of affairs which are quite different from those supported by modal counterparts of the same sentence. Statements of possibility like *It's {possible, somewhat likely} that the butler is the culprit* do not support inferences that are entailed by the non-modal sentence, e.g., that the butler lied to the police when he said he was innocent. Automatically distinguishing between the actual and the modal is necessary for high-quality textual entailment (Burchardt and Frank 2006, Saurí and Pustejovsky 2007, Hickl and Bensley 2007), information extraction (Karttunen and Zaenen 2005), question answering (Saurí et al. 2006), sentiment analysis (Wiebe et al. 2005), and machine translation (Baker et al. 2012). The special attention that modality and non-factuality have received in the context of the textual entailment task is evidence that these aspects of meaning cannot be ignored by practical applications that seek to approximate a complete understanding of text.

From a computational perspective, modally-annotated corpora are an indispensible resource for training systems to automatically interpret modality. This includes automatically detecting modal expressions in text, classifying them into types (as will be described shortly below), identifying their semantic scope, and so on. Theoretical linguists have turned to modal annotation as well, both as a resource for obtaining detailed descriptions of how modality is expressed—within and across languages, and through the historical development of languages—and in order to test the predictions of formal semantic theories of modality (de Haan 2012a, Hacquard and Wellwood 2012, Yanovich 2012).

The annotation of modal meaning is not an easy task. It presents a variety of challenges, relating on the one hand to the practicalities of annotation and on the other to the subtlety of distinctions to be drawn in the modal domain. The very definition of the set of modal words raises questions about the differences between prototypical exemplars of the class (e.g., *should, can*) and verbs of propositional attitude (e.g., *believe, want*). Modals also tend to be highly ambiguous, with senses that are subtly distinct and overlapping (Kratzer 1981). Their interpretation essentially presents a challenge of Word Sense Disambiguation: *A ten-year-old can drive that truck* can be interpreted both as describing what is sanctioned by law (a deontic use of *can*), and as describing an ability of certain individuals (an ability use of the modal). In a given context, one interpretation (or **modality type**) but not the other may be intended. Mitigating contextual pressures, it has been argued that the syntactic configuration in which a modal appears constrains the range of interpretations it can receive (Cinque 1999, Hacquard 2006). The complex interaction of context, grammar, and lexical content in the expression of modal meaning makes the task of creating high-quality annotated modal corpora particularly important and challenging.

Our aim in the current project is to propose and evaluate a comprehensive and language-independent schema for annotating modality. We experiment with annotating modality types at different levels of granularity, marking up textual spans that describe the **backgrounds** of modal statements (in the sense of Kratzer 1981), as well as comparative and gradable modal expressions. These features are described in detail in Section 3. In the next section, we situate our project in the context of related work.

2 Previous Annotation Efforts

Recent years have seen a number of major efforts of annotating modal expressions in corpora. The majority of these works have targeted English texts (see Table 1 for a snapshot), but there are also notable projects on other languages (de Haan 2012b, Hendrickx et al. 2012). We briefly summarize these representative studies below.

In English, annotation of modality has focused to a large extent just on modal auxiliaries and verbs. Aspects of modal interpretation that have received the most attention concern the proposition in the scope of a modal (Ruppenhofer and Rehbein 2012, Hendrickx et al. for Portuguese), whether or not it occurs in the scope of a negative operator (de Haan 2011, Baker et al. 2012; also much related work on event factuality and sentiment analysis), the source providing the modal background (Ruppenhofer and Rehbein 2012, Hendrickx et al. 2012) and the interpretation of the modal as either epistemic or non-epistemic (i.e., “root”). Hacquard and Wellwood (2012) focus specifically on modals that occur in embedded environments (antecedents of conditionals, questions, and complements of attitude verbs); de Haan (2011, 2012a) correlates the interpretation of modals with register (written versus spoken), grammatical features of their subject (e.g., its person specification), and properties of their verbal complement (e.g., its temporal inflection).

Baker et al.	**Words**	~150 lemmas
	Types	Non-standard (success, effort, intention, ability, belief, and certain root modalities)
	Texts	Written
	# tokens	229
de Haan	**Words**	*must* (and others)
	Types	Root/epistemic
	Texts	Written, spoken
	# tokens	1508 (141)
Hacquard & Wellwood	**Words**	*must, have to*
	Types	Root/epistemic
	Texts	Written
	# tokens	2426
Ruppenhofer & Rehbein	**Words**	*must, ought, shall/should can/could, may/might*
	Types	Epistemic, deontic, dynamic, optative, concessive, conditional
	Texts	Written
	# tokens	1162

Table 1: Recent annotation of modality in English

3 Annotation Task and Proposed Schema

3.1 Overview

With the long-term goal of comparing our annotations to previous work, ultimately producing a resource that is both reliable and built on a platform that is widely used in the field, we followed Ruppenhofer and Rehbein (2012) and chose the MPQA corpus (Wiebe et al. 2005; Wilson 2008) as the corpus to be annotated.

In defining the targets for annotation, we developed a working definition of what counts as modal. This definition was intended to apply not just to modal auxiliaries and verbs (e.g., the typically-targeted *must, have to*), and, moreover, to distinguish modals from closely related attitude verbs. A **modal expression** according to this definition is (i) an expression used to describe alternative ways the world could be, (ii) that has some sort of propositional argument (referred to as the **prejacent**),[1] and (iii) is not associated with an overt attitude holder. Only expressions that met all three criteria were considered modal targets for our annotation. For example, while the noun *hope* is considered a modal in *There is* ***hope*** *that she will win*, it is not considered a modal in *There was still* ***hope*** (condition (ii) is not met). Similarly, *believed* counts as a modal in a sentence like *It is* ***believed*** *that…*, but not when it has an attitude holder as its subject (e.g., in *She* ***believes*** *that…*).

To make the annotators' task of identifying every modal expression in a text more manageable, a seed list of expressions was generated. The list was used to pre-highlight candidate modal targets in the documents to be annotated. It was compiled according to the procedure in (1) and contained a total of 321 lemmas.

(1) Seed list – lemmas of expressions in (i)-(iv):

i. Adjectives retrieved via the corpus query `[it is [ADJ] that]` in a large corpus (ukWaC, Ferraresi 2007)
ii. Modal expressions annotated in previous work (Table 1)
iii. Synonyms of the expressions in (i), gathered manually using a thesaurus
iv. Modal adverbs, nouns, comparative and superlative adjectives related derivationally to the expressions in (i)-(iii)

Importantly, annotators were instructed to mark every expression that conveyed modality, thereby adding to the pre-highlighted items, and to delete items that were marked in error. Excluded expressions included future *will*, modals in idiomatic phrases (for example, *better* in *the sooner the better*), conditional *should* (as in *Should it be possible, do it!* or *If the negotiations should continue*), and certain teleological verbs (in particular, *aim at/to* in which an attitude holder or goal expression are explicit).

The task was carried out by two annotators. We began with a training round of 40 files, during which the annotators raised issues and discussed problematic cases among themselves and with a larger group of experts. At the end of the training phase the annotation guidelines had been finalized. In total, the annotators completed 200 files (183 of which contained at least one modal target according to at least one annotator). These included 1232 fully annotated targets that both annotators agreed were modal and that had identical spans. There was considerable disagreement concerning what counts as modal, as can be seen in Table 2.

Annotator 1	1605
Annotator 2	1810
Total agreed modal	1232

Table 2: Number of tokens annotated

3.2 Tool

We used the MMAX2 tool (Müller and Strube 2006) for our annotation, following Hendrickx et al.'s positive experience. In addition to its relatively user-friendly graphical interface, MMAX2 can accommodate annotation of overlapping and discontinuous elements. As noted by these authors, these abilities are crucial for annotation of modal features (see (7) below for an example involving a discontinuous prejacent).

[1] An exception are adnominal modal adjectives. See discussion of Modified Elements below.

Figure 1 shows a target modal as it appears to the annotator in MMAX2. Connecting lines are drawn between the modal and spans of text that correspond to its prejacent, and other features potentially represented in the text.

Figure 1: Modal target *can* annotated in MMAX2. One line connects the modal to its Prejacent, and a second one connects it to its Background.

3.3 Annotated Features

This section presents our annotation schema. We discuss the central features of the schema, focusing on those that are new to this project: Modality Type (coarse-grained and fine-grained), Propositional Arguments (including prejacents and comparatives), Background, Modified Element, Degree Indicator, and Outscoping Quantifier. More detailed descriptions of all features appear in the annotation guidelines, which will be made available separately.[2]

Modality Type. Every modal was categorized on two levels with respect to the type of modality it conveyed in context. Seven fine-grained types were distinguished: Epistemic, Circumstantial, Ability, Deontic, Bouletic, Teleological, and Bouletic/Teleological. However, before this classification was made, annotators first categorized each modal as belonging to one of three coarse-grained categories: Epistemic or Circumstantial, Ability or Circumstantial, and Priority. The label **priority** picks out a conceptually motivated subclass of non-epistemic modalities: those that use some "priority" (a desire, a goal) to designate certain possibilities as better than others (Portner 2009:135ff.)[3] In Section 4 we show that annotators reliably agreed on only the highest level split between priority and non-priority interpretations.

Non-priority

- *Epistemic*: the claim is based on evidence, belief or knowledge.
- *Circumstantial*: the claim is based on circumstances.
- *Ability:* the claim is based on what someone/something can do.

(2)

a. Mary ***must*** have a good reason for being late. (Epistemic)

b. … for we were in the little salon where Madame never sat in the evening, and where it was by mere ***chance*** that heat was still lingering in the stove. [Web] (Circumstantial)

c. The potential losses that could be incurred by the tourist industry following a major disaster ***can*** be illustrated by examining the consequences of hurricanes Luis and Marilyn to the Caribbean island of Anguilla in 1995. [Web] (Ability)

In cases of ambiguity, annotators were instructed to mark the modality type on the fine-grained level as Ability/Circumstantial (interpreted as both ability and circumstantial) or Epistemic/Circumstantial, as appropriate. Another special use of the Ability/Circumstantial label was reserved for opportunity modals (for example, the interpretation of *can* in *You can see the ocean through this window*).

(3)

a. "…but I say: Please, that is the most dangerous thing you ***can*** ever do," he said. [MPQA] (Ability/Circumstantial)

b. Temperatures are very ***likely*** to be significantly higher when in full screen mode because your graphics card will be running in 3D mode. [Web] (Epistemic/Circumstantial)

Priority

- *Deontic*: the claim is based on rules, standards, (social) norms.
- *Bouletic:* the claim is based on someone's wishes or desires.
- *Teleological:* the claim is goal-oriented.
- *Bouletic/Teleological*: for tokens that are arguably both bouletic and teleological.

---

[2] Examples from the ukWaC corpus are noted below as [Web], and ones from the annotated corpus are noted as [MPQA].

[3] A special category of "TBD" (to-be-discussed) was available for annotators to mark unclear examples that should be revisited. This category was only used a handful of times.

(4)

a. The rich ***must*** give money to the poor. (Deontic)

b. Today, he is being completely isolated and the ***desire*** to drive him away is scarcely disguised. [MPQA] (Bouletic)

c. The owner and a neighbor who had helped him put down the animal were sent ***urgently*** to the Hospital for Infectious Diseases in Miercurea Ciuc, where they received preventive anti-rabies treatment. [MPQA] (Teleological)

d. The donors' conference, [...], was hoping to raise 1.25 billion dollars (1.47 billion euros) for Yugoslavia this year for ***urgent*** repairs to infrastructure and salaries to teachers and other civil servants. [MPQA] (Bouletic/Teleological)

In cases of an ambiguity between deontic and any other priority-type modality, a modal was given the Priority subtype (the same label as its coarse-grained classification).

(5)

When it gets to the point that Northern Alliance troops start firing in the air just next to a car with reporters, you ***have to*** do something about it, " said Cordell. [MPQA] (ambiguous Priority)

In addition to modality type, every target modal was also specified for its environment's polarity and associated with a prejacent in the text.

Environmental Polarity. The environment of the modal was set to 'positive' by default. In cases where the modal was in a semantically downward entailing environment, the value of the feature was changed to 'negative' and the item creating the negative environment (e.g., *not* or *reject*) marked in the text. In cases where modals were in the scope of multiple negative words, these were all marked.

(6)

"There ***could*** be <u>no</u> expediency, <u>no</u> compromise, <u>no</u> lapse in vigilance," he said." [MPQA]

Note that the environment of the modal was not affected by the modal's internal polarity: an inherently negative modal such as *unlikely* does not create a negative environment. Also, not every combination of a modal with negation results in a negative environmental polarity for the modal (e.g. *should* in *should not* outscopes the negation).

Propositional Arguments. The textual span corresponding to the proposition a modal applies to was annotated as the modal's prejacent. Prejacents excluded non-restrictive relative clauses and parentheticals, tense markers (*is* in (7)), expletive *it* (see (7)), markers of environmental polarity, and degree indicators (see below).

(7)

It is ***likely*** <u>that John</u>, who was my upstairs neighbor, <u>will run the race</u>.

Determining whether temporal adverbials fell within the prejacent of the modal was left to annotator discretion.

(8)

According to military experts, it is ***possible*** <u>that clashes will resume between the Taleban and UIFSA forces in various regions of Afghanistan in the next few days and weeks</u>. [MPQA]

As modals may also be used comparatively, annotators could mark when a modal appeared in equative, comparative, or superlative forms. In these instances, prejacents as well as *than*-clauses in the text were associated with the modal.

(9)

a. It is ***likelier*** <u>that John will run a race</u>. (Comparative; the prejacent is underlined and there is no *than*-clause)

b. <u>John</u> is as ***likely*** <u>to run a race</u> as <u>HE</u> is <u>TO CLIMB A MOUNTAIN</u>. (Equitive; Prejacent and than-clause underlined, the latter in small caps)

The remaining features are independent of the modal, thus they were only marked if they appeared in the text.

Source. This feature was designed to indicate the entity that had the ability or knowledge that are the basis for a modal claim, or in the case of priority modals, the entity placing the obligation or setting the goal that the modal takes into account. (This definition of Source is similar to the one proposed by Hendrickx et al. 2012 and Ruppenhofer and Rehbein 2012). Annotators marked the closest instance of reference to the source, pronominal or otherwise. Sources could be inanimate.

(10)
In his latest speech, Chen said the long-standing dispute with China ***must*** be resolved through dialogue with respect to the principles of democracy and freedom. [MPQA] (Deontic Source)

Where two or more possible sources were detected, as in (11), no Source was marked.[4]

(11)
Chang said after visiting Chinese communities in the United States, New Zealand and Southeast Asia that education and cultural work ***needs*** to be further strengthened in the Chinese communities in Southeast Asia. [MPQA]

Background. The background of a modal is a sequence of (one or more) constituents that provide a textual description of the circumstances and/or priorities that the modal claim is based on.[5] The background may be expressed in an adjunct that contains a description of a relevant situation; in the case of a priority modal, (12), a rationale clause may describe the relevant goals and preferences.

(12)
With the new method, all you ***need*** do to get an answer is put all the ingredients into a test tube, mix them together, and check to see what the output is. [MPQA]

Modified Element. We also included in our annotation modals that were not used predicatively, but as modifiers of nouns or adjectives (as in, *the* ***probable*** *answer*, *It was* ***sufficiently*** concrete). The head (underlined in the examples above) of the modified phrase was marked as a Modified Element and associated with the modal in these cases.[6]

Degree Indicator. Any item that indicated degrees of modal necessity or possibility was annotated. In cases where two or more degree indicators were used, they were treated as one degree indicator for purposes of the annotation.

(13)
There is a very high ***likelihood*** that it will rain.

Adverbs like *perhaps* were not treated as degree indicators, but as independent modals (in cases such as *It could perhaps be...*).

Outscoping Quantifier. Quantificational elements that are part of a modal's prejacent but are nevertheless interpreted as taking semantic scope over the modal were marked as outscoping quantifiers.

(14)
Everyone ***can*** win the prize.

Finally, additional features for each modal were its **Lemma** (included automatically for pre-highlighted modals), and a text box for optional comments (used, e.g., for indicating that the modal was in the title of the document). Table 3 summarizes the features annotated and their possible values.

Feature	Possible Values
Modality type (coarse)	Epistemic or Circumstantial, Ability or Circumstantial, Priority
Modality type (fine)	Epistemic, Circumstantial, Ability, Deontic, Bouletic, Teleological, Bouletic/Teleological
Environmental polarity	Positive, Negative
Propositional arguments	textual span(s)
Source	textual span

[4] An alternative strategy would be to mark multiple Sources in such cases, or to mark the more plausible source (in this example, *Chang*).
[5] A related feature tracking whether there is "overt evidence" for a *must* claim in the text is raised by de Haan (2011).

[6] The phrase modified by the modal (e.g., *repairs to infrastructure* in (4d)) was marked as the modal's prejacent.

Background	textual span
Modified element	textual span
Degree indicator	textual span
Outscoping quantifier	textual span
Lemma	free text
Additional notes	free text

Table 3: Annotated features and their values

4 Reliability of the Annotations

As an indication of the reliability of our annotation, we measured inter-annotator agreement on the following features: Modality Type, Prejacent, and Background. The results obtained allow for initial comparison with previous annotation projects.

4.1 Inter-annotator Reliability Measure: Krippendorff's α

Inter-annotator reliability is standardly measured with a number of different α and κ scores (Carletta 1996, Artstein and Poesio 2008). These scores measure the degree of agreement for a pair or set of annotators given some common set of annotation guidelines. Though the details of calculation and presupposed conditions vary among different scores, the statistics themselves are comparable, with 0.0 reflecting agreement no better than would occur at chance and 1.0 reflecting perfect agreement.

Many reliability measures presuppose identical annotation items. In our case, this is insufficient, as the annotators are marking features with values that are spans of text of potentially variable position and length (e.g., Prejacent, Background). For this reason, Krippendorff's (2004) α score was selected as a measure of inter-annotator reliability. The agreement score is computed along a continuum, comparing the overlap between spans that were marked by the annotators, and allowing for partial agreement when spans are not perfectly aligned.

In our analysis, we included only the 1232 agreed-upon modals (targets that were marked as modal by both annotators and that had identical spans). We ignored cases of partial overlap (where one annotator marked *would like* and the other its substring *would*, for example). We calculated inter-annotator agreement on Modality Type, Prejacent (to the exclusion of other propositional arguments), and Background.

4.2 Results

Table 4 shows the reliability of annotations for the three features mentioned above. We begin with discussion of Modality Type, the feature that has received most attention in previous work. The basic score, measuring agreement on the ten possible values for this feature, was low (α = 0.49). The effect of a number of category collapses was therefore investigated. First, all priority-type categories were collapsed (i.e., Bouletic, Teleological, Bouletic/Teleological, Deontic, and Priority were treated as one category for purposes of the agreement calculation; "Priority types collapsed" in Table 4). Second, all non-priority types (i.e., Epistemic, Circumstantial, Ability, Epistemic/Circumstantial, Ability/Circumstantial) were collapsed into one, and finally, both of these collapses were applied together. This final merging of categories (the final row in the Table) resulted in a high α score of 0.89.

Conventionally, κ and α scores are considered acceptable at a threshold of 0.80 (Carletta 1996). A word sense disambiguation task (Ng et al. 1999) has been reported with raw κ scores at 0.317, and 0.862 after using a collapsing algorithm to attain better agreement. Hacquard and Wellwood (2012) achieved a κ score of 0.84 on a two-way classification of epistemic versus root modalities. Table 5 compares our α agreement scores for individual modals with the κ scores reported on a superset of the data by Ruppenhofer and Rehbein ([RR 2012] below).

Feature: Modality Type	α
No collapse	0.49
Priority types collapsed	0.66
Non-priority types collapsed	0.73
Priority vs. Non-priority	0.89
Feature: Prejacent	0.65
Feature: Background	0.61

Table 4: Inter-annotator reliability scores

	Items	**Raw α**	**Non-P collapsed**	**P collapsed**	**Priority vs Non-priority**	**[RR 2012] κ**
may, might	102	0.27	1.00	N/A	1.00	0.621
must	140	0.40	0.40	0.90	0.90	0.848
shall, should[7]	140	0.23	0.31	0.71	0.80	0.602
can	238	0.34	0.90	0.35	0.91	0.614

Table 5: Modality Type agreement by word

Agreement scores for the Prejacent and Background features, α = 0.65 and α = 0.61 respectively, represent how well the spans that annotators marked align overall (although note that they do not take into account the association of particular spans to modals in the text). Prejacents have been annotated in previous studies, but inter-annotator agreement scores for this feature have not previously been reported, as far as we know.

4.3 Discussion

Collapsing the priority types as well as the non-priority types results in essentially a two-way distinction that is similar to the Root versus Epistemic distinction assumed in previous annotation projects (see Table 1). Our results support making the distinction at this coarse-grained level. Since the α score is designed to cancel out any random (dis)agreement, the increasing values with each collapse show that the annotators cannot reliably discern the more fine-grained distinctions of modal "flavor". (Rubinstein et al. 2012 report similar results in a crowdsourcing experiment with non-expert native speakers.) Nevertheless, while the coarse-grained distinctions may prove more reliable for Machine Learning and other NLP applications, having access to the annotators' finer-grained judgments could be helpful for theoretical purposes. They allow the researcher to distinguish between more and less ambiguous exemplars of each modality type and to investigate the grammatical and contextual properties of examples that are judged as more ambiguous. We thus propose to annotate for each modal a unique coarse-grained type as well as a list of one or more fine-grained types corresponding to the annotators' individual judgments.

Since collapsing non-priority subtypes results in a greater increase to the 0.49 α baseline (0.73 vs. 0.66 for priority collapsed), we conclude that the difficulty to distinguish epistemic, circumstantial, and ability modalities is greater than the difficulty to distinguish between different subtypes of priority modality. In the confusion matrix below, the affinity between the ability and circumstantial types is evident in the decisions of row annotator within the **a**-column, and in the decisions of column annotator across the **c**-row.

	a	**a+c**	**e+c**	**e**	**c**	**b**	**b+t**	**t**	**d**	**p**
a	55	4	1	7	6	0	1	0	0	0
a+c	2	1	0	0	1	0	0	0	0	0
e+c	0	0	0	6	2	0	0	0	1	0
e	1	1	8	139	30	0	0	1	10	0
c	87	23	20	110	176	0	0	12	18	3
b	0	0	0	2	2	4	2	1	1	2
b+t	0	0	0	5	3	9	1	2	4	5
t	11	2	1	16	27	4	4	102	76	35
d	11	1	0	7	2	0	0	3	126	3
p	1	1	0	0	0	0	1	1	24	4

Table 6: Modality Type confusion matrix (**a**-ability, **c**-circumstantial, **b**-bouletic, **d**-deontic, **e**-epistemic, **p**-priority, **t**-teleological, **a+c**-ability and circumstantial, similarly **e+c** and **b+t**)

Cells marked in red in the confusion matrix evidence confusion between teleological and deontic interpretations on the one hand, and epistemic/circumstantial and even ability interpretations on the other. We leave investigation of the relevant examples to future work.

5 Conclusion

We have proposed a schema for annotating modal meaning that builds on previous work and extends it with a number of novel features. Completing the annotation of the MPQA corpus according to this schema, we hope to contribute to the development of reliable computational resources for detecting and interpreting modals in naturally occurring text.

Acknowledgments

This research was funded by National Science Foundation grant BCS-1053038, "The Semantics of Gradable Modal Expressions", to Graham Katz, Paul Portner, and Elena Herburger.

[7] No instance of *shall* was tagged by both our annotators.

References

Ron Artstein and Massimo Poesio. 2008. Inter-coder agreement for computational linguistics. Extended version of an article in *Computational Linguistics*.

Kathryn Baker, Michael Bloodgood, Bonnie J. Dorr, Chris Callison-Burch, Nathaniel W. Filardo, Christine Piatko, Lori Levin, and Scott Miller. 2012. Use of modality and negation in semantically-informed syntactic MT. *Computational Linguistics* 38(2):1-28.

Aljoscha Burchardt and Anette Frank. 2006. Approaching textual entailment with LFG and FrameNet frames. In *Proceedings of the Second PASCAL Challenges Workshop on Recognising Textual Entailment (RTE-2)*.

Jean Carletta. 1996. Assessing agreement on classification tasks: The kappa statistic. *Computational Linguistics* 22(2): 249-245.

Guglielmo Cinque. 1999. *Adverbs and functional heads*. Oxford University Press.

Adriano Ferraresi. 2007. Building a very large corpus of English obtained by Web crawling: ukWaC. MA Thesis, University of Bologna.

Ferdinand de Haan. 2011. Disambiguating modals: constructions and *must*. Ms.

Ferdinand de Haan. 2012a. The relevance of constructions for the interpretation of modal meaning: The case of *must*. *English Studies* 93(6): 700-728.

Ferdinand de Haan. 2012b. Automatic disambiguation of modals and evidentials: A corpus-based investigation. Slides of talk presented at the conference "The Nature of Evidentiality", Leiden University, June.

Valentine Hacquard. 2006. Aspects of modality. Doctoral Dissertation, MIT.

Valentine Hacquard and Alexis Wellwood. 2012. Embedding epistemic modals in English: A corpus-based study. *Semantics and Pragmatics* 5:1-29.

Iris Hendrickx, Amália Mendes and Silvia Mencarelli. 2012. Modality in text: A proposal for corpus annotation. In *Proceedings of the Eight International Conference on Language Resources and Evaluation (LREC'12)*.

Andrew Hickl and Jeremy Bensley. 2007. A discourse commitment-based framework for recognizing textual entailment. In *Proceedings of the workshop on textual entailment and paraphrasing*.

Lauri Karttunen and Annie Zaenen. 2005. Veridicity. In *Dagstuhl seminar proceedings. Annotating, extracting and reasoning about time and events*, ed. G. Katz, J. Pustejovsky, and F. Schilder.

Angelika Kratzer. 1981. The notional category of modality. In *Words, worlds, and contexts*, ed. H.-J. Eikmeyer, H. Rieser, 38-74. Walter de Gruyter.

Klaus Krippendorff. 2004. Measuring the reliability of qualitative text analysis data. Annenberg School for Communication Department Papers, University of Pennsylvania.

Hwee Tou Ng, Chung Yong Lim, and Shou King Foo. 1999. A case study on inter-annotator agreement for Word Sense Disambiguation. In *Proceedings of the Siglex-ACL Workshop on Standarizing Lexical Resources*.

Christoph Müller and Michael Strube. 2006. Multi-Level Annotation of Linguistic Data with MMAX2. In *Corpus Technology and Language Pedagogy. New Resources, New Tools, New Methods*, ed. S. Braun, K. Kohn, J. Mukherjee, 197-214. Peter Lang.

Paul Portner. 2009. *Modality*. Oxford University Press.

Aynat Rubinstein, Dan Simonson, Joo Chung, Hillary Harner, Graham Katz, and Paul Portner. 2012. Developing a methodology for modality type annotations on a large scale. Slides of talk presented at the Modality Workshop, Ottawa University, April.

Josep Ruppenhofer and Ines Rehbein. 2012. Yes we can!? Annotating English modal verbs. In *Proceedings of the Eight International Conference on Language Resources and Evaluation (LREC'12)*.

Roser Saurí and James Pustejovsky. 2007. Determining modality and factuality for textual entailment. In *ICSC-07*.

Roser Saurí, Marc Verhagen and James Pustejovsky. 2006. Annotating and recognizing event modality in text. In *19th International FLAIRS conference (FLAIRS 2006)*.

Janyce Wiebe, Theresa Wilson, and Claire Cardie. 2005. Annotating expressions of opinions and emotions in language. *Language Resources and Evaluation*, 37(2-3):165-210.

Theresa Wilson. 2008. Fine-grained subjectivity analysis. Doctoral Dissertation, University of Pittsburgh.

Igor Yanovich. 2012. Possibility or collapse on the path to necessity? Slides of talk presented at Georgetown University, November.

Distant annotation of Chinese tense and modality

Nianwen Xue, Yuchen Zhang and Yaqin Yang
Computer Science Department
Brandeis University, Waltham, USA
{xuen,yuchenz,yaqin}@brandeis.edu

Abstract

In this paper we describe a "distant annotation" method by which we mark up tense and modality of Chinese eventualities via a word-aligned parallel corpus. We first map Chinese verbs to their English counterpart via word alignment, and then annotate the resulting English text spans with coarse-grained tense and modality categories that we believe apply to both English and Chinese. Because English has richer morpho-syntactic indicators for tense and modality than Chinese, we hope this distant annotation approach will yield more consistent annotation than if we annotate the Chinese side directly. We report experimental results that show this expectation is largely borne out.

1 Introduction

It is often the case that linguistic information that is hidden in one language is directly observable in another. This is particularly true for typologically distant language pairs. For example, tense and number are "invisible" in languages like Chinese but they are explicitly marked in languages like English where there is a more developed morphological system. In English, for example, tense is grammaticalized as an inflectional morpheme attached to a verb. In Chinese, on the other hand, such morphological cues are rare or non-existent, and the underlying semantic tense has to be inferred from the context. (1) is an example Chinese sentence and its verb 举行 ("hold") has no morphological inflections of tense. However, a notional semantic tense that indicates the temporal location of the event denoted by 举行 can be inferred by the time expression 明年 ("next year").

(1) 大会 明年 在新加坡 举行 。
conference next year in Singapore hold .

"The conference will be held in Singapore next year."

In this paper, we describe a method of annotating the tense of a Chinese sentence by annotating the tense of its English translation and then projecting this annotation back onto the Chinese sentence. Specifically, we identify all English text spans that are aligned to a Chinese verb in a word-aligned parallel Chinese-English corpus. Then all the English text spans will be annotated with tense and modality. Note that the resulting English text spans after such mapping may not necessarily be English verbs because a Chinese verb may be translated into an English noun, or words of other parts-of-speech. In (2), for example, "appointment" is translated into a Chinese verb "赴约". Nevertheless, such English text spans can still be treated as "anchors" of tense and modality. Our hypothesis is that we are more likely to obtain consistent annotation by annotating the English translation rather than the Chinese source directly because the morpho-syntactic cues in English are good indicators of tense and they constrain the choices that an annotator has to make during the annotation process.

(2) a. One day in August 2005 , Abather was driving Balqes , six months pregnant with their second child , to a doctor 's appointment .

b. 2005年8月的一天，阿巴舍正开车送怀着他们第二个孩子已有六个月的巴尔科斯赴约 去医生处。

It is important to note that the target of our annotation is the underlying semantic tense, not the grammatical tense. The semantic tense can be interpreted as a relation between the time that an event occurs and a reference time in the sense of (Reichenbach, 1947). In a written text, this reference time is usually the time when the document is created or the time when another event occurs. This relation does not change regardless of whether it has a morpho-syntactic manifestation when a sentence is translated into a different language.

The grammatical tense, indicated by the morpho-syntactic cues, do not always have a one-to-one correspondence with the semantic tense. In English, it has long been noted that the same surface morpho-syntactic form may indicate very different underlying semantic notions of tense (Dinsmore, 1991; Cutrer, 1994; Fauconnier, 2007). For example, the morpho-syntactic form "are playing" in both (3a) and (3b) indicates present progressive tense, but underlyingly, while in (3a), the present tense indeed indicates a *present* time, in (3b), the present tense indicates a *future* time. Typically, however, these morpho-syntactic cues have a relatively straightforward correspondence with their underlying semantics in the source language, making the manual annotation of the underlying semantics very straightforward.

(3) a. They are playing soccer in the park.
b. They are playing soccer next Tuesday.

In addition to the "polysemous" finite tense forms, there are also a large proportion of English verbs that appear in non-finite forms, which can also be construed as having multiple semantic tense values. The examples in (4) show that infinitives and gerunds can indicate past (4a, 4b), present (4c,4d) or future (4e,4f) times. When projected onto a target language, these non-finite forms need to be disambiguated so that the correct semantic tense can be accurately inferred from the context in the target language.

(4) a. I enjoyed reading the book.
b. The prisoner managed to escape.
c. I enjoy reading.
d. To err is human, to forgive is divine.
e. The prisoner is considering escaping.
f. The prisoner hopes to escape tomorrow.

Tense is intricately related to modality. Although both (3b) and (4f) indicate future times, they differ in that (3b) indicates an event that has been previously scheduled to happen while (4f) describes an intended event that may or may not materialize. There is a higher level of certainty that the soccer playing event is going to happen than that escaping event will. In other words, although the tense is the same, the modality, which accounts for the degree of certainty of an event, is different.

The rest of the paper is organized as follows. In Section 2, we describe our annotation framework. We present the results of a preliminary annotation experiment in Section 3. Section 4 describes related work and Section 5 concludes the paper.

2 Specifications

As described in Section 1, each Chinese verb instance is mapped to a text span in English and then annotation is performed on English text by labeling these text spans with tense and modality categories. Each text span is annotated along three dimensions to support the planned automatic inference of tense and modality on the Chinese side. The first dimension is the *semantic tense*, and the annotator must indicate whether the text span describes a past, present, or future event state. The second dimension is *event type* that indicates whether the text span represents a habitual event, an ongoing event, a completed event, an episodic event, or a state. The event type is annotated because it has been shown (Smith, 2001; Smith and Erbaugh, 2005; Xue, 2008) that in a language without explicit tense markers, event types are good indicators of tense. The third dimension is *modality*. The modality dimension is broadly construed and it classifies events or states as actual, intended (which encompasses expected, planned events), hypothetical (as in conditional clauses) or modalized. An event or state is modalized if it occurs with a modal verb that indicates possibility, necessity, or ability. These categories are very coarse-grained and we did not get into the finer distinctions of different types of modality. Each of these categories are described in greater detail below and illustrated with examples.

When annotating the semantic tense, some of events or states cannot be interpreted in relation to the document creation time and we have to annotate its relative tense. In such cases, we also link this text span to another that it depends on for its temporal interpretation. These links are all in the direction from the *dependent* text span to its *head* span. Such dependent text spans are typically tagged with one of the relative tense categories that include *Relative Present*, *Relative Past* or *Relative Future* when annotating *tense*.

As a practical matter, we also need to determine whether a text span needs to be annotated for all three dimensions in the first place. In (5a), for example, text spans that consist entirely of auxiliary verbs do not need to be annotated if they are followed by a main predicate and the tense and modality annotation will be associated with the main predicate. In (5b), the text span is a modal verb, and modal verbs only need to be annotated for tense, but not for event type and modality. In some cases, a verb as part of a Chinese verb compound is mapped to an adverbial particle or a preposition in English and such particles or prepositions need not to be annotated as the tense and modality is attached to the main verb in the compound. An example is given in (5c), and the main verb is italicized and the preposition is underlined.

(5) a. Six months after the kidnapping , he still had n't *gotten the surgery* he needed to heal his burned flesh.

b. You can make a contribution at : International Catholic Migration Commission Citibank USA 153 East 53rd Street , 16th floor New York, NY 10043 .

c. Very few organizations are working on *getting* aid to Iraqi refugees.

2.1 Tense

We set up six categories for semantic tense, and these are *past*, *present*, *future*, *relative past*, *relative present*, and *relative future*. The relative tense categories are inspired by the discussions of tense in (Comrie, 1985), and they are triggered by verbs in non-finite forms that have a clear dominating verb ("head verb" in dependency structure terms) that it depends on for its temporal interpretation. A link will also be annotated between the dependent verb and its head verb. The annotation of links will be discussed in greater detail in Section 2.4. Each of these six categories are defined and illustrated below. The relevant text spans are underlined.

Past The text span describes an event or state that happened in the past.

(6) He started an engineering firm and worked with contractors such as ABB and Kellogg , Brown and Root;

Present The text span describes a present event or state. This includes a present state, an event that happens repeatedly in the present, a present on-going event, a completed event that has present relevance.

(7) It is centered on the Hongshui River hydroelectric plant .

Future The text span describes an event that will happen in the future, or a future state.

(8) Some people will prefer that option because it 's more convenient .

Relative Past The text span describes an event that happened in the past, or a past state relative to the event it depends on. In (9),"crossing" happened before the time "repeated" happened, i.e. "crossing" is relatively past to "repeated".

(9) After crossing a 30 - foot no man's land we *repeated* the process at the second wall .

Relative Present The text span describes an event that happens in the present, or a present state relative to the event it depends on. In (10),"taking up" happens at the same time with "'ve got", i.e. "taking up" happens at the present relative to "'ve got".

(10) I *'ve got* two dead monitors taking up space in my office .

Relative Future The text span describes an event that happens in the future or a future state relative to the event it depends on. In (11a), "to strengthen" depends on "has invested" for its temporal interpretation, and "to create" depends on "to strengthen". In (11b), "to be listed" depends on "approved" and the former logically occurs after the latter.

(11) a. It *has invested* more than 130 billion yuan to strengthen the construction of infrastructures and basic industries so as to create a sound environment for expanding the opening up to the outside world . (link from "to strengthen" to "has invested", from "create" to "has invested", and from "for expanding" to "create")

b. Among them , 57 items *were approved* to be listed in the national , provincial and municipal Torch Plan and their quantity ratio is tops among the new , high level technology industry zones of the entire country .

Even in English, annotating tense can be challenging in at least two scenarios, and the first one being when there is a mismatch between the grammatical tense and the semantic tense. In (12), for example, "reaches" has a grammatical present tense, but it should be interpreted an event that occurs in the future. In this case, the grammatical tense can be deceiving and can be an impediment that prevents the annotator from making the correct decision. The other scenario is when the text span is a verb that takes on a non-finite form of a verb (13a) or other grammatical categories such as nouns (13b) and adjectives (13c). When this happens, tense is grammatically under-specified even in English, just like in Chinese. In this case, the temporal interpretation of the event depends on the larger context rather than the event denoting verb itself. While event denoting verbs in non-finite forms such as infinitives and participles can be annotated with a relative tense with a link to its dominating verb, event denoting nouns and adjectives often do not have one single dominating event that it can get its temporal interpretation from. Therefore, for nouns and adjectives as well as participle forms modifying nouns, we do not annotate relative tense. Instead, we assign an absolute tense value that reflects the temporal interpretation of the event based on the context of the event. In (13b), for example, "acquittal" gets a past tense due to clues like "since", and "conviction" gets a past interpretation due to the fact that it has a temporal modifier "1999", which makes the temporal location of "conviction" explicit. In (13c), "rich" and "doting" are adjectives that modify nouns, and their temporal interpretation comes from the verb "appeared". These adjectives are translated from predicative adjectives in relative clauses in Chinese, which can also be interpreted for tense based on the larger context.

(12) To ensure that the money reaches the Iraqi program , write Iraq - icmc on your check.

(13) a. This should be a motif familiar to anyone acquainted with the literature of mind control and ritual abuse survivors : the father and first controller , passing his child - victim up the social ladder of abuse in return for status , protection and reward .

b. He ' s moved on since his aquittal , like Gary Glitter did after his 1999 conviction , having departed last June for a Bahrain " vacation " from which he ' s yet to emerge .

c. For the people working at Bahrain ' s malls , the person covered head to toe in a black veil , gloves and glasses appeared to be a rich , doting Saudi mother.

2.2 Eventuality Type

We define five eventuality types, and these are *habitual event*, *state*, *on-going event*, *completed event*, and *episodic event*. The eventuality type is set up as a way to help infer tense. Habitual events, on-going events, and states, for example, tend to occur in the present by default, while episodic events tend to occur in the past by default (Smith and Erbaugh, 2005). Given that there is no grammatical tense in Chinese, such a classification may prove to be an important source of information that helps predict tense. Each of the five types is described and illustrated below, and the relevant text spans are underlined:

Habitual Event The text span describes an event that happens repeatedly on a regular basis (14a, 14b). Habitual events are compatible with adverbial modifiers such as "often", "usually", "rarely","generally", "seldom", etc. Habitual events describe a pattern of actual events. General truths and statements also belong to this category (14c,14d).

(14) a. I used to drive to work but now I take the bus.

b. At present , the Pu Kang Company , which produces the vaccine in this zone , has already formed a production scale of 5 million doses per year .

c. Time flies.

d. The moon travels around the earth.

State The text span describes an unchanging situation that will continue unless something happens to change it.

(15) a. It is centered on the Hongshui River hydroelectric plant .

b. but the demand far outstrips the money available to us , says Magy Mahrous , who oversees the project.

c. According to investigation , each enterprise entering this zone has one or more new , high level technology projects or products .

On-going Event The text span describes an event that is on-going. The progressive aspect marker is generally a good indicator of this type of event.

(16) a. At the school, where Bush was reading a story to a group of second-graders, the news came on TV that a second jet had hit the World Trade Center .

b. God is testing us , he said .

Episodic Event The text span describes a situation that involves some sort of change or occurrence.

(17) a. The National Weather Service reported that two other tornadoes touched down in the region - one in east Lindale, another in southeast Calhoun.

b. Gross domestic product, the broadest measure of the nation's economic growth, contracted at an annual rate of 0.1% from October to December, the Commerce Department said Wednesday.

Completed Event The text span describes a past event that has present relevance.

(18) Within three to five years , Beihai has constructed the framework of a modernized city.

2.3 Modality

This dimension is used to distinguish events that actually happens from events that are intended, expected, possible, required, hypothetical. We define four modality categories – *actual event* is for events that actually happens, while non-actual event types include *intended event*, *hypothetical event*, and *modalized event*. These are described and illustrated below:

Actual Event The text span describes an event or state in the real world that actually happened, happens, is happening or will happen. This includes habitual events that happen repeatedly, or negated event that actually do not happen.

(19) Beihai has already become a bright star arising from China 's policy of opening up to the outside world .

Intended Event The text span describes an intended or expected event or state that does not necessarily happen or hold in the real world. This covers events that are intended, expected, planned, etc. An intended event typically follows a main verb and denotes the purpose or intention of the main verb. Those text spans are typically verbs in non-finite forms and are linked to a main verb that occurs before or after it. Text spans following modal verbs are excluded from this category, and are put into *Modalized event* category.

(20) a. It has also drafted three documents for attracting foreign capital , strengthening horizontal economic integration and allowing more authority for foreign operations .

b. Among them , 57 items were approved to be listed in the national , provincial and municipal Torch Plan and their quantity ratio is tops among the new , high level technology industry zones of the entire country .

Hypothetical Event The text span describes an event or state that is in a conditional (e.g., if, when) clause or takes place conditional on something else, and does not necessarily happen in reality.

(21) Would the experiment have been as successful if they had not spent the money ?

Modalized Event The text span follows a modal verb, and describes a possible or necessary event or state, or an ability.

(22) a. The recent confrontation could ignite regional convulsions as Turkey is sucked into Syria, leading to belated actions from the international community.

b. That now will not happen, but it is possible that he could be summoned by Congress to testify later.

Our annotation scheme for modality as it currently stands is still very coarse-grained. For example, we do not distinguish the different types of modalities traditionally introduced by modal verbs, such as epistemic and deontic modals. The classification is also shallow in that our intent is to simply identify syntactic constructions that have a modal interpretation. For instance, the sentences in (23) definitely expresses uncertainty, but because they are not associated with one of the above syntactic constructions, they are still considered to be "actual", which is the default category for modality.

(23) a. It will probably rain tomorrow.

b. It will possibly rain tomorrow.

2.4 Links

The annotation of links is triggered by events expressed by verbs in non-finite forms that have a clear dominating (head) verb. The annotation of links is closely tied to the annotation of relative tense. When an event is annotated with a relative tense category, a link is annotated so that the relative tense of the dependent event can be interpreted in relation to the temporal location of the dominating verb. The link is always in the direction from a dependent text span to a head text span.

(24) a. To further expand the opening up to the outside and promote outwardly economic development , Guangxi has come up with a series of policies to make use of foreign investments .

b. This development zone is located in the downtown area of Hangzhou , a famous Chinese scenic sightseeing city , and is a national level new , high level technology industry development zone approved for construction by the State Council in 1991 .

In (24a), "expand" and "promote" are both linked to "has come up with", with relative future tense assigned to the first two spans. In (24b), "for construction" is annotated with a relative future tense and linked to "approved".

3 Annotation Experiments

As of this writing, we have completed the first round of our annotation experiments. We selected 50 sentences, which consist of 944 words, from the Parallel Aligned TreeBank (Li et al., 2012) from the LDC. There are 167 text spans that are marked up as event anchors. The annotation experiment involves three annotators. Each sentence is annotated three times and we computed their pairwise agreement statistics. The results of the average agreement scores are presented in Table 1:

	Tense	Event Type	Modality
Agreements	78.6% (131/167)	73.5% (123/167)	81.4% (136/167)
Kappa scores	0.71	0.65	0.70

Table 1: Inter-annotator agreement

It is premature to draw any firm conclusions about the effectiveness of this distant annotation approach with this first round of annotation, but it is worth noting that the inter-annotator agreement statistics are already comparable with and even better than that reported in (Xue et al., 2008) where tense is directly annotated on Chinese text using annotators that have undergone significant training and there were a smaller number of tense categories (four). We believe this shows the initial promise of this approach. From the statistics in Table 1, we can also see that our annotators show better agreement for Modality and Tense than Eventuality Type. We analyzed our annotation results through confusion matrices which show that the most difficult distinction for Tense is between *Present* and *Future*, and the confusion happens mostly on modal verbs, modalized events and hypothetical events, where it is difficult to distinguish these two tenses. The most challenging distinction for Eventuality is between *Habituals* and *State*, indicating that the distinction between those tags is still vague and not clearly defined.

4 Related Work

In a series of TempEval evaluations (Verhagen et al., 2007; Verhagen et al., 2010) that are aimed at detecting time expressions, events and the relations among them, (abstract) tense determination is formulated as a task of determining the relation between an event and the document creation time. TempEval uses a fairly coarse-grained set of values (Before, Before or overlap, Overlap, After, After or Overlap) to represent abstract "tense". The "tense" annotation task in the TempEval evaluations targets the main event of a sentence, while we are attempting to annotate the semantic tense for all eventualities, including events and states in non-finite verb forms or even in nominal forms. We also define an *event type* classification that is intended to help infer tense, mindful of the fact that there will not be morpho-syntactic cues on the Chinese side that can help make such determination. We also attempt to set up a fairly coarse-grained classification system for modality of events. Tense, aspect, and modality are also annotated in the TimeBank (Pustejovsky et al., 2005) as attributes of events, but TimeBank generally annotates the grammatical tense of English verbs. For example, the tense of an event that takes the form of a non-finite verb or a noun will get the value of "None" even though the semantic tense for some non-finite verbs can be determined, as shown in (4). We target the semantic tense instead of the grammatical tense because we think they are "transportable" across languages. Our ultimate goal is to infer the semantic tense on the Chinese side, not just on the English side.

A recent attempt to annotate and disambiguate the semantic tense for English is by Reichart and Rappoport (2010), who introduced a more general Tense Sense Disambiguation (TSD) task that provides a fine-grained sense taxonomy for tense. They view tense as having three different levels: Concrete (surface) Syntactic Forms (CSF, e.g., am/is/are V-ing), Abstract Syntactic Forms (ASF, e.g., present progressive), and a taxonomy of 103 different underlying senses. For example, Reichart and Rappoport define 11 underlying senses for the "simple present" ASF which include "things that are always true", "general and repeated actions and habits", "plans, expectations and hopes". These fall under the scope of modality in theoretical linguistics research (Kratzer, 1981; Carlson and Pelletier, 1995; Guéron and Lecarme, 2008). Reichart and Rappoport essentially use modality as a semantic dimension to disambiguate the different "senses" of abstract tense forms. Their goal is to predict the underlying senses given the surface CSFs. We target similar distinctions in our annotation, but instead of treating these distinctions as unstructured fine-grained senses, we classify events along three different dimensions that in conjunction can make similar distinctions in a more structured manner.

On the Chinese side, there have been several past attempts to infer "tense" for Chinese automatically using statistical models and modest success has been reported. There are two general approaches to "tense" inference for Chinese. The first approach has been to manually annotate tense on Chinese verbs (Ye et al., 2006; Ye, 2007; Xue et al., 2008; Xue, 2008) and use the annotated data to train statistical models to predict tense in previously unseen text. (Xue, 2008) has shown that even though there are no morpho-syntactic clues for tense in Chinese, contextual information can be exploited to infer "tense". Such contextual information includes explicit clues such as time expressions and aspect markers as well as implicit information such as verb types: bounded events (e.g., "explode") tend to occur in the past while unbounded events tend to occur in the present (e.g., "believe, know, like"), a generalization first articulated in (Smith and Erbaugh, 2005). Maintaining consistency among annotators when annotating a phenomenon with a total lack of explicit surface cues, however, proved to be a very challenging task. (Xue et al., 2008) reported an inter-annotator agreement of 75% despite of using a fairly coarse-grained tagset (Xue et al., 2008), a result that is comparable to that of our first round of annotation. The second approach is cross-lingual projection and this is the tack that Liu et al (2011) took. They mapped grammatical tense in English onto Chinese via word-aligned parallel text. The issue with mapping the surface grammatical tense is that, as we discussed above, the syntactic forms of tense are ambiguous with regard to their underlying semantics. As a result, when they are projected onto a different language, the same context will point to different grammatical tense categories. This will confuse the statistical machine learning models and hamper their performance and hence limit the utility of the resulting automatic systems.

We believe that our distant annotation approach combines the best of both worlds. Unlike manual annotation on just the target language (Chinese) side, we benefit from the presence of the morpho-syntactic cues in the source language (English). Effectively, our distant annotation approach allows us to annotate the underlying semantics of tense in the easier source language and map it to the more difficult target language. At the same time, unlike direct projection of surface forms of tense, our distant annotation approach maps the surface forms to an underlying semantic representation that is free from language-specfic idiosyncracies at the morpho-syntactic level.

5 Conclusions and Future Work

We describe a distant annotation approach for annotating the tense, event type and modality of events in Chinese text by annotating their English counterpart via a word-aligned parallel corpus. Preliminary results indicate that this approach shows promise as an effective alternative to annotating the Chinese text directly, a challenging task since Chinese does not have the morpho-syntatic cues that constrain annotation choices. We are currently performing additional annotation experiments while refining our annotation guidelines. The ultimate goal is to generate consistently annotated data on the Chinese side that can be used to train statistical models to automatically predict tense, event type and modality of Chinese events. We believe such a tool would benefit a wide variety of natural language applications that include Machine Translation and Information Extraction.

Acknowledgment

This work is supported by the IIS Division of National Science Foundation via Grant No. 0910532 entitled "Richer Representations for Machine Translation" . All views expressed in this paper are those of the authors and do not necessarily represent the view of the National Science Foundation.

References

Gregory N. Carlson and Francis Jeffry Pelletier. 1995. *The Generic Book*. Chicago: University of Chicago Press.

Bernard Comrie. 1985. *Tense*. Cambridge University Press.

Michelle Cutrer. 1994. *Time and Tense in Narratives and Everyday Language*. Ph.D. thesis, University of California in San Diego.

John Dinsmore. 1991. *Partitioned Representations*. Dordrecht, Netherlands: Kluwer.

Gilles Fauconnier. 2007. Mental Spaces. In Dirk Geeraerts and Hubert Guyckens, editors, *The Oxford Handbook of Cognitive Linguistics*.

Jacqueline Guéron and Jacqueline Lecarme. 2008. *Time and Modality*. Springer.

Angelika Kratzer. 1981. The notional category of Modality. In H.J. Eikmeyer and H. Rieser, editors, *Words, Worlds and Contexts*. Berlin: de Gruyter.

Xuansong Li, Stephanie Strassel, Stephen Grimes, Safa Ismael, Mohamed Maamouri, Ann Bies, and Nianwen Xue. 2012. Parallel Aligned Treebanks at LDC: New Challenges Interfacing Existing Infrastructures. In *Proceedings of LREC-2012*, Istanbul, Turkey.

Feifan Liu, Fei Liu, and Yang Liu. 2011. Learning from chinese-english parallel data for chinese tense prediction. In *Proceedings of the 5th International Conference on Natural Language Processing*, pages 1116–1124, November.

James Pustejovsky, Bob Ingria, Roser Sauri, Jose Castano, Jessica Littman, Rob Gaizauskas, Andrea Setzer, G. Katz, and I. Mani. 2005. The specification language TimeML. In I. Mani, J. Pustejovsky, and R. Gaizauskas, editors, *The Language of Time: a Reader*. Oxford University Press.

Roi Reichart and Ari Rappoport. 2010. Tense sense disambiguation: A new syntactic polysemy task. In *Proceedings of the 2010 Conference on Empirical Methods in Natural Language Processing*, pages 325–334, Cambridge, MA, October. Association for Computational Linguistics.

Hans Reichenbach. 1947. *Elements of Symbolic Logic*. The MacMillan Company, New York.

Carlota S. Smith and Mary Erbaugh. 2005. Temporal interpretation in Mandarin Chinese. *Linguistics*, 43(4):713–756.

Carlota Smith. 2001. Discourse modes: Aspectual and tense interpretation. In J. Busquets, F. Lambert, and A. Le Draoulec, editors, *Cahiers de Grammaire 26: Sémantique et Discours*. ERSS et Université de Toulouse-le Mirail, Toulouse.

Marc Verhagen, Robert Gaizauskas, Frank Schilder, Mark Hepple, Graham Katz, and James Pustejovsky. 2007. Semeval-2007 task 15: Tempeval temporal relation identification. In *Proceedings of the Fourth International Workshop on Semantic Evaluations (SemEval-2007)*, pages 75–80, Prague, Czech Republic, June. Association for Computational Linguistics.

Marc Verhagen, Roser Sauri, Tommaso Caselli, and James Pustejovsky. 2010. Semeval-2010 task 13: Tempeval-2. In *Proceedings of the 5th International Workshop on Semantic Evaluation*, pages 57–62, Uppsala, Sweden, July. Association for Computational Linguistics.

Nianwen Xue, Zhong Hua, and Kai-Yun Chen. 2008. Annotating tense in a tenseless language. In *Proceedings of the Fifth International Conference on Language Resources and Evaluation*, Marrakech, Morocco.

Nianwen Xue. 2008. Automatic Inference of the Temporal Location of Situations in Chinese Text. In *EMNLP-2008*, Honolulu, Hawaii.

Yang Ye, Victoria Li Fossum, and Steven Abney. 2006. Latent features in automatic tense translation between Chinese and English. In *The Proceedings of the 5th SIGHAN Workshop on Chinese Language Processing*, Sydney, Australia.

Yang Ye. 2007. *Automatica Tense and Aspect Translation between Chinese and English*. Ph.D. thesis, University of Michigan.